The

CRUISING
WOMAN'S

Advisor

How to Prepare for the Voyaging Life

Diana Jessie

International Marine
Camden, Maine

International Marine/
Ragged Mountain Press

A Division of The McGraw·Hill Companies

10 9 8 7 6 5 4 3 2

Library of Congress Cataloging-in-Publication Data available.

Questions regarding the content of this book should be addressed to:
International Marine
P.O. Box 220
Camden, ME 04843

Questions regarding the ordering of this book should be addressed to:
The McGraw-Hill Companies
Customer Service Department
P.O. Box 547
Blacklick, OH 43004
Retail customers: 1-800-262-4729
Bookstores: 1-800-722-4726

The Cruising Woman's Advisor is set in 10 pt. Electra with old style numerals.

Photograph of Lin Pardey on page xx by Helen J. Meier
Photograph of Lael Morgan on page xix by Richard Veoz

Printed by R.R. Donelley, Crawfordsville, Indiana
Design and Production by Dan Kirchoff
Edited by John Kettlewell; Kathryn Mallien; Jonathan Eaton;
    Cynthia Flanagan Goss

For the cruising gypsies,
who possess little
and are the richest women
in the world,
and the good men
with whom they sail

"Rough Waters"

Sometimes I ask myself
What am I doing here
Madly subjecting me
To great discomfort and fear?

We're sailing inside
A washing machine
That's producing more foam
Than any soap I've seen

Not a moment's
Peace or rest we find
Our muscles stiff
And sore with time

[All complaining aside
The reason that I ride
Is to feel more of life
More alive inside!]

Excerpted with permission from
Just Cut the Lines and Go,
by Janet E. Davis,
Owner/Skipper, Mystical

Contents

FOREWORD BY LIN PARDEY X
PREFACE XII
INTRODUCTION XIV
PARTICIPANTS XVI

1 — The Cruising Life 1
    What Is the Cruising Lifestyle? 2
    Why We Go 3
    Demands and Rewards 5

2 — His Dream, Her Dream, Too 8
    The Raison d'Etre 8
    Cruising Roles and Relationships 9
    Communication Required 11
    Living the Dream 12

3 — Getting Started 14
    Where Do I Learn? 15
        Your Mate as Your Instructor 16
        Sailing Schools 17
        Learning on Your Own 19
    Do I Have to Become an Expert? 21
    What Do I Need to Learn? 21
    If My Partner Falls Overboard, How Do I Rescue Him? 22
    How Can I Go Cruising When I Always Get Seasick? 23
    How Do I Keep the Boat from Heeling? 23
    How Do You Live in Such a Confined Space? 23
    How Do You Manage the Boat on Long Voyages? 24
    What Scares You Most About Voyaging? 24
    How Many Storms Have You Encountered at Sea? 24
    How Often Do You Go Home? 25

4 —A Boat for Just the Two of Us 26

The Right Boat 28
    A Personal Choice 29
    Sailing Venue 30
Size 30
How Does It Sail? 31
Living Space 31
    Bunks 32
    The Galley 32
    The Head 33
    Adequate Stowage 34
Boat Gear 34
Safety Gear 36
Upkeep 38

5 —Fearing the Weather Ahead 39

Weren't You Scared? 40
Gathering Information 41
Learning to Cope 42
Steering Clear of Bad Weather 44
    Pilot Charts, a Basic Tool 44
What Do You Do to Prepare for Bad Weather? 45
    Equipment 45
    Discomfort 46
    Practice 47
The Silver Lining 48

6 —Pirates and Protection 49

Isn't It Dangerous Out There? 49
There Are Some Real Dangers 51
How Do We Protect Ourselves? 52
    Traveling in Company 53
    Carrying Weapons 53
    Attention-Getting Goods Aboard 54
    Other Things You Can Do 54
    My Own Approach 55

7 —In Sickness and in Health 57

Medical Preparation and Planning 58
    Training 58
    Medical Kit 59
    Medical Records 60
    Health Insurance 61
    Help and Emergencies 62
Medical Concerns 63
    Seasickness 63
    Menstrual Cycle 64

Pregnancy 65
Menopause 66
Skin Protection 67
Fitness 68

8 — Children On Board 70
Infants and Toddlers 71
Preparing Your Boat 72
Safety Issues 72
Health Concerns 73
Diapers 74
Food 74
Social Life 75
School-Age Children 76
Education Underway 76
Health and Safety for Kids on the Go 77
Food for Growing Children 77
Quarters for Kids 78
Getting Along 78
Adolescents 79
Health and Safety for Teens 80
A Place of Their Own 80
High School and Beyond 80

9 — Folks at Home 82
Preparation 82
Communicating After You Leave 84
Your Feelings 84
Family Issues and Events 85
Becoming a Grandparent 85
Disasters at Home 86
Emergency Contact 86
They Don't Want Me to Go 87
Guilt 88

10 — Staying in Touch 90
Who Forwards the Mail and Pays the Bills? 90
Mail 92
A Deliverable Address 93
Communication with Radios 94
Amateur Radio Operators (Hams) 95
Telephone Communication 95
Communication in the Future 96

11 — Career Planning and Employment 98
The Option of Timing 99
Expectations 99

Combining Work and Play 100
    When is Recess? 101
Sabbatical Cruising 102
Making a New Career 103
    On-the-Water Professionals 103
    Peddling Your Skills 105
Constraints and Regulations 106

12 — Home Is Where the Heart Is 107

Your Boat is Your Home 107
    Boat Units 108
    Great Things Come in Small Packages 108
Moving Aboard 109
Selecting the Systems 109
    The KISS Principle 109
    What Are the Choices? 110
Comfort Comes in All Shapes 111
I Don't Need It 112
Your Home Is Your Nest 113

13 — Memories and Mementos 115

Inventory Reduction 115
    I Might Need That 116
Keeping Valuables 117
What's Worth Keeping? 117
    Pick Something Small 117
    Make a Choice 118
Saving Important Items 118
    Homebase Storage 118
    Borrowed Storage 119
    Safety Deposit Box Storage 119
New Mementos 119
Disposal Systems 121

14 — Twenty-Four Hours a Day 123

A Different Pace 123
Schedules for Sailing 125
    Standing Watch 125
    Off Watch 126
    Nets 127
    Weatherfax 127
Time at Anchor 128
    Everyday Life in Port 128
Destinations 129
    Making Friends 130
    Friends from Home 131
Will I Be Bored? 132

15—Woman to Woman 133

Bathing 133
Hair Care 135
Skin Care and Makeup 136
Clothing 137
Sex at Sea 138

16—Making the Most of It 140

Things to Learn for Independence 141
    Dinghy Operation 141
    Speaking the Language 142
Grow as You Go 142
    Cruising Skills 143
    Personal Skills 144
Smell the Roses 146

17—A Few Words About Provisioning 147

Provisioning for Cruising 147
Shopping in Foreign Countries 149
What's Out There 150
Foreign Finds 152
Bright Copper Kettles 153
Tableware 155
Stowage 155

EPILOGUE—The Voyage Continues 158

APPENDIX—RESOURCES FOR CRUISING SERVICES
    AND INFORMATION 160
BIBLIOGRAPHY—RECOMMENDED READING FOR CONFIDENCE
    AND PREPARATION 164
INDEX 166

Foreword

by Lin Pardey

It is 1987. We are at our home base in New Zealand, *Taleisin* swinging to her mooring just beyond the windows. Three women, with seven circumnavigations and who knows how many thousands of miles under their belts, sit cross-legged on a bunk, talking of lives dominated by voyaging. Susan Hiscock recalls her most worrisome moments, aground in the Torres Straits, dozens of miles from the nearest settlement—the story turns hilarious as she tells of a boatload of missionaries happening by. Their assistance turned a possible disaster into a great story. "Eric always told people he'd *truly been saved*," she quips. Patience Wales, on her second circumnavigation, tells of the drama created by trying to be both a roving magazine editor and a voyager as she explored the communicationless, exotic outer Solomon Islands. Then I can't help but add my most worrisome moments—when amazing 100-mile-per-day currents swept us past Japan.

As I listened to our concerns back in 1987 I remember thinking how different they were from those of people (women, especially) who are first contemplating a cruising life. Like Diana Jessie, I have been in front of groups of women who asked each and every one of the questions covered in this book.

Although my answers to some questions may have been different in detail to those you read here, this reflects only differences in lifestyle or cruising style. For example, because we rarely cruise with crew, we carry sufficient water and have special facilities for luxurious (by cruising standards) showers on a daily basis at sea; because Larry and I dislike telephones and went cruising to avoid them, naturally we also avoid transmitting radios.

But the information Diana offers is not only useful and accurate, it also stresses an often ignored fact that the 1987 intimate meeting of three longterm cruising women illustrated for me — cruising is a participation sport. The more both partners get involved, the larger the rewards. Furthermore, sailing and the amazingly simple but efficient floating machine you will live on provide the key to exploring the world on an enjoyable, affordable long-term basis.

Diana will, as you read her well-organized ideas, encourage you and your mate to become more knowledgeable about your sailing home and conveyance; more aware of its inherent sail-powered reliability and its hidden pleasures.

No book, no seminar, can answer every question you may have — and when you finish this book you'll probably still wonder, "Should I go cruising, will I find it fulfilling, fun, exciting? Is it worth the risk?"

Diana Jessie definitely feels it is. I'm still looking forward to the next sailing adventure, the next landfall after thirty years of voyaging. Each long-term voyager we meet seems completely comfortable with the only possible answer to those really big questions. By choosing to avoid risk, you may be taking the biggest risk of all.

—*Lin Pardey, Hong Kong, 1997*

Preface

When I returned from a seven-year, 60,000-mile circumnavigation with my husband, we presented seminars, on our own initiative and with the sponsorship of *Cruising World*, for would-be cruisers who wanted to share in what we had learned.

We undertook a seminar tour and traveled thousands of miles and talked to thousands of people in the ensuing three years. Although our audiences were mostly made up of couples, the women seemed reluctant to ask questions during the opening sessions. At the first break, however, I would be surrounded by women full of questions about cruising. They wanted to know more about leaving home, fear, personal care, raising children, and other issues. It was clear there were topics women wanted to discuss that were not addressed in our agenda.

My husband and I revised our program, much to the satisfaction of all participants, and this book has grown from my encounters with women who wanted to learn about cruising.

In researching *The Cruising Woman's Advisor*, I interviewed cruising women with a broad range of perspectives on the cruising lifestyle, so this book has more than one point of view. I extend my thanks to these women who graciously shared their experiences and advice. I learned from them, and, at the same time, renewed old friendships and made new ones. Nancy Jewhurst went beyond the call by eagerly and enthusiastically reading rough drafts while anchored in Zihuatanejo, Mexico. Her encouragement kept me on track.

This book would not have seen the light of day without the support and confidence of John Kettlewell, Kate Mallien, and Jon Eaton of International Marine. They led me through the maze of word processing formats and rewrites with great patience. Migael Scherer, Nancy

C. Hauswald, Nikki Perryman, and Lynda Childress, managing editor of *Cruising World* magazine, offered enlightened and useful critiques to help me manage the scope of this book.

Finally, my cruising lifestyle and the joy it brings would not be complete without my husband Jim. He survived the writing of this book with great patience and self-control, for he was not privy to the manuscript's contents until it was complete. His strength, skill, and humor make him a great partner—wherever the wind may take us.

Introduction

Women who are cruising seek each other out and use every opportunity to talk with one another about personal matters. We talk about coping with the unknown, gaining a better understanding of our boats, and improving our relationships with our husbands (or male partners) and the family we left at home. We talk candidly, even if we do not know each others' last names, because we share a bond in cruising.

This book brings those conversations to a wider audience. It was written to encourage and support women at all stages of their cruising lives: from those who are dreaming about cruising to those who have already left. This book was also written for the man who wants a woman to go cruising with him and wants to understand her concerns.

I interviewed twenty-one cruising women in the process of writing this book, talking with them everywhere from the Pacific Isles to boat shows in big cities. Their insights into the cruising lifestyle are the backbone of this book. They are a diverse group with a wide range of experience. Some have sailed around the world and survived historic storms. Some have raised and schooled their children on board. Some have created lives with room for careers and homes and cruising. In the following pages, first-time cruisers and old hands, new moms and grandmothers, women who are married, divorced, single, and widowed, and professional and recreational sailors all address the physical, emotional, and practical concerns cruising women share.

The scope of this book is broad, but each chapter pinpoints specific areas. For first-time sailors, there is basic information about the cruising lifestyle and sailing skills. For women who are ready to make longer trips, there are chapters on what kinds of boat and equipment to consider and how to deal with the weather. There is advice for women making a full-time commitment to cruising and giving up jobs and homes and raising children on board. For those who expect to spend extended time in foreign countries, there are chapters about staying in touch and taking care of your health and personal safety.

A brief biography of each cruiser interviewed is included in the section titled Participants. I have only brushed the surface of their accomplishments. I encourage you to read their books and articles and the stories written about them. If you have the chance to meet any of these women at seminars, lectures, or boat shows, don't miss the opportunity.

These women have made cruising more than a hobby: They've made it a lifestyle. The reasons they cruise, the experiences they've had, and the problems they've had to solve will reassure you that cruising is exciting and rewarding. Whether you want to know how to leave your career or how to bathe in two cups of water, I hope the answers will entertain and enlighten you.

Participants

 Gail Amesbury lives with her husband, Don, in Florida. Their three children were educated at boarding schools in England and spent holidays cruising with their parents. After cruising in Europe, Africa, and the Caribbean, Gail and Don sold their boat and settled down to watch their children become established and independent. They hope to get a new boat and continue their voyage soon.

 Nancy Bischoff is cruising in the Pacific with her husband, Kurt, and their two sons on board a Tayana 37. The boys grew up on the boat and are now experiencing life as young cruisers. Teenagers frequently are alienated from their families, but the Bischoffs are proof that parents and children can remain close as children grow older. Nancy and Kurt see their voyage as a gift to their sons.

 Gail Bowdish, M.D., is an emergency medical specialist based in a city hospital in Minnesota. She races her Islander 36 on the Great Lakes. As a doctor and sailor, she is knowledgeable about the health concerns women have while cruising in areas far away from immediate help. She provides helpful advice on several important health matters.

 Louise Burke started sailing with her husband in 1968 and worked with him taking guests on charterboats and delivering boats from port to port. After her husband's death, she acquired her captain's license in 1973 and continued to skipper charterboats and go racing. In 1976 Louise became the sailing master of *Mistral*, an 82-foot Herreshoff schooner sailing out of the United States Naval Academy, and the first woman to teach sailing at the school. She also served as the assistant director and coach of the varsity offshore sailing team, which included twenty-four boats and 109 midshipmen to make the program the largest one of its kind. Today she sails out of Annapolis, Maryland, and Marblehead, Massachusetts, and is an active lecturer and consultant.

 Barbara Colborn started sailing in her thirties with her husband, David, on a MacGregor 26. They put their boat on a trailer and hauled it to different parts of the country to sail. Chartering in the Caribbean got them interested in going cruising. They bought a 38-foot boat and in 1994 began their first long cruise. They cruised for fourteen months, traveling to Mexico, the Hawaiian islands, and back to California. New to cruising, Barbara offers a fresh and positive perspective. She has self-published two books about her experience: *A Sailor's Devotional* and *Crossing the Horizon: One Couple's Mid-Life Adventure*. She is looking forward to cruising again.

 Paula Dinius is a survivor of the infamous Queen's Birthday Storm, which struck a group of boats sailing from New Zealand to Tonga in June 1994. The book *Rescue in the Pacific* by Tony Farrington (International Marine, 1996) is the story of the storm and its survivors and is must reading for all cruisers. When her husband, Dana, was severely injured, they abandoned their boat to be rescued. Later the boat was salvaged and subsequently was lost in a fire. Paula and Dana are currently enjoying a rural lifestyle and their baby girl. Their long-range plans include returning to the sea.

 Réanne Hemingway-Douglass wrote the amazing book *Cape Horn: One Man's Dream, One Woman's Nightmare* (Fine Edge Productions, 1994) more than twenty years after making that passage. Her candor about the experience, and about her family relationships during the voyage, is bold and informative. Still married and still adventurous, she and her husband own Fine Edge, a small publishing company; they hope to produce another book soon about Patagonia and Cape Horn. Réanne and her husband cruise the Pacific Northwest each summer in their diesel trawler.

 Lura Francis and her husband Jack circumnavigated in a 32-foot boat that they finished themselves. She was plagued with major health problems for nearly ten years before going cruising, but that did not deter her from realizing the cruising dream she and her husband shared. Shortly after returning from their voyage and retiring to their mountain home, Jack died of a heart attack. Lura, an artist, is now in her mid-sixties, living alone, and still painting. Her joy and pride in the voyage she and Jack took together brings a sparkle to her eyes.

 Irene Hampshire is in her thirties and raising two sons on a small boat in southern California. Most of her cruising time is spent helping her mate, John Shampain, deliver boats to different ports and race them. She believes cruising is the best way to travel. She also has deep feelings about raising children in today's world. Her long-range plans include moving back to land life, someday.

 Nancy Jewhurst is cruising full time on board a Traveler 32 with her husband, Victor, and her son, Kyle. She exudes enthusiasm about cruising because she believes the lifestyle gives her a closeness with her family that might not be possible in any other kind of life. Just entering her forties, she is a model for women considering rearing their children while cruising. She expects to be land based later in life if her parents need her assistance.

Barbara Marrett is a contributing editor to *Cruising World* magazine. She and John Neal sailed the South Pacific extensively in his Hallberg-Rassy 31, and they have provided many entertaining hours to audiences around the country with their lectures on cruising. They published an account of their experiences in *Mahina Tiare* (Pacific International Publishing, 1993). Barbara is land based now, but she still manages to sail much of each year.

Patricia Miller is a licensed skipper who delivers yachts between East Coast and West Coast ports in the United States via the Panama Canal. Her first cruises included some bad times, but she has since become more skilled and independent as a sailor. She is an editor and journalist and co-author of *The Boating Guide to Mexico* (Situr Marinas, 1995) with her husband John Rains. Patricia combines work, cruising, and caring for her mother.

Lael Morgan is an accomplished photographer, author, and scholar. She currently chairs the Department of Journalism and Broadcasting at the University of Alaska, Fairbanks. Her cruise from Boston, through the Panama Canal, and up to Alaska in the early 1960s was the basis for her first book, *Woman's Guide to Boating and Cooking* (Dodd Mead, 1968). She and then-husband Dodge made this long trip without the sophisticated electronics and onboard comforts available to cruisers today, but she still recalls her early experiences with great enthusiasm.

Pat Nolan operates a sailing school in the Virgin Islands and began her sailing career in Seattle. There, she was active in the Seattle Women's Sailing Association and served as the organization's president in 1987. She is a strong advocate for women's sailing and is eager to help women find a place in the sport, as racers or as cruisers. Her theory on how women differ from men in their approach to sailing is an important contribution to the chapter on sailing skills.

Lin Pardey has been cruising for more than thirty years with her husband Larry. Unlike most modern cruisers, the Pardeys built a small wooden boat (29'6") and sailed her without an engine. They circumnavigated in a 24-foot boat named *Serafyn* before building their larger boat, *Taleisin*. Lin has been cruising most of her adult life and she is practical and forthright in her comments. She has written and co-written with Larry several definitive books on cruising, including their latest, *Storm Tactics Handbook* (Pardey Books, 1995). Lin contributed the foreword for this book.

Nancy Payson fell in love with a man who promised to show her the world. She married Herb, and he kept his promise. Starting with little experience and learning as she sailed, Nancy has become an accomplished sailor. She is also about to publish her own cookbook. Nancy is the epitome of what cruisers hope to be when they cruise: happy, warm, vital, and strong. Nancy and Herb share a monthly column in *Sail* magazine.

Suzanne Pogell founded Womanship, the first sailing school for and by women, in 1984. She based the program on a concept, teaching approach, and curriculum designed to give adult women hands-on opportunities to discover the joys of sailing and to gain and advance real skill and the confidence to take charge. The Womanship program has been hailed by *Practical Sailor* as one of the two best sailing schools in the country; the school now teaches in twelve locations around the world. Suzanne writes and lectures extensively on marketing to women and on ways to begin and advance sailing skill and confidence.

Dawn Riley is the most notable woman sailor in America, having taken part in two America's Cup campaigns and two Whitbread Round-the-World Races. She comments on sailing as she knows it and about starting at an early age to gain the independence she needed to take her to the top. Her book *Taking the Helm* (Little, Brown and Company, 1995) is a great story of her experience skippering sixty-foot *Heineken* and its all-female crew in the 1993–1994 Whitbread race. Dawn lives part time in New Zealand.

Migael Scherer is the author of *A Cruising Guide to Puget Sound* (International Marine, 1995). For twenty years, her cruising ground has stretched from Seattle to southeastern Alaska. Her special contribution to this book is describing how you can cruise, live, and work as a liveaboard. The 50-foot ketch she and her husband built is a satisfying place to live and work.

Michelle Simon, M.D., is a pediatrician in Maryland and an enthusiastic sailor. She is a strong advocate for women in sailing and for women's health. She offers advice about caring for children while cruising to assist those who are considering entering the cruising life with the whole family. Divorced and sailing, she looks forward to working with cruisers and helping them plan their healthcare.

Patience Wales, editor of *Sail* magazine, has circumnavigated twice. Her view of cruising has not changed over the years, although her taste in boats has. She offers encouragement and direction on learning to sail, coping with fear, and gaining independence as a cruiser. She anticipates cruising in decadent comfort with the completion of her next boat.

1

The Cruising Life

WHEN THE YOUNG WOMAN sitting next to me on the plane discovered that I lived on a boat and spent my life sailing, she asked me how I slept, cooked, bathed, shopped, and worked—as if I had just arrived from Mars. When we parted, she told me that she could not imagine what my life was like, but that it sounded perfect.

Most people do not understand what it's like to live and cruise on a sailboat, and their curiosity and amazement is always entertaining. They first try to understand the cruising life in the same day-to-day terms that define their lives. What is it like to live without a car, without a telephone, without daily contact with the rest of the world? But what is important to know goes beyond those day-to-day details. Cruisers' lives may seem as alien as life in outer-space. But there is great joy in cruising. It is a life of adventure, challenge, and independence.

If you are considering becoming a cruiser, I am sure your questions are endless: What is cruising really like? Can I do it? Will I like it? Will it be horrible, or wonderful? Women who have cruised along coastlines and across oceans, on big boats and small, for long periods of time and for short spans, all asked those same questions before they left.

What Is the Cruising Lifestyle?

There is no single definition of the cruising lifestyle. The answer depends on who you ask, for one of the best things about cruising is that it is a way of living that can be approached and managed in many different ways.

For me, cruising is the simple life. I live on a boat instead of living in a house or in an apartment. My possessions are few, and my living space is smaller than a mobile home's. I do not spend hours cleaning, talking on the phone, or watching television. I share every day—in fact, nearly every minute—with my husband in this same space. We live day to day, planning what we want to do and where we want to go each day. It is rare that we use the phrase, "I have to . . . " unless I am writing or the weather is bad.

We do not own suitcases because we take our home with us wherever we go, and we never have jet lag. Our dinghy is our "car" when we want to go ashore. We have no faxes, phones, or beepers on the boat, so people either communicate with us face to face or wait for us to turn on our radio.

Our boat is the focus of our lives. It is our home and our mode of transportation, and it holds everything we own. Whenever I have to be away from the boat, I am always anxious to return.

Cruising means moving from place to place. Some cruisers move from port to port, some cross oceans, and some travel around the world. The neighborhood changes constantly, and there is always a new place to visit, something new to learn, and new people to meet.

You may think cruising is a lonely life because you are always sailing away from people. But you meet people living the same life as you. You meet on docks and in anchorages, and you become friends because you share this unique lifestyle. As bluewater cruiser Nancy Payson says, "Your entertainment comes from friends and books, sharing with friends the adventures that you have."

Change is part of a cruising life. If you look forward to change, you will see cruising as an adventure. Lin Pardey says, "If you want adventure and freedom, I think you have to give up the perception of comfort and safety. There is no such thing as security in life. The only thing in life that's positive is change, so why not get out there and enjoy it? Accept change, and you can enjoy cruising."

Not everyone who cruises crosses an ocean or becomes a circumnavigator. Many cruisers live on board full time and cruise coastal areas. Migael Scherer has lived on her boat in Puget Sound and cruised the

Pacific Northwest and southeast Alaska for twenty years. For her, cruising is not unlike being a career tourist. It is "spending time on a hook somewhere and then moving on to another place. You send yourself on a prolonged vacation. I like to be a long-term tourist. I want to be part of communities. Knowing people is important to me. A year is too short a time. It satisfies me to stay several years, then move."

Cruising does not have to be a permanent lifestyle. Combining a land life with cruising is the only way some couples and families can cruise. Cruising for a year may be their limit because they want to keep their children in school. They may have only a short sabbatical from work. They may have a limited budget and cannot stay away from land life and careers for too long. Some cruisers do not plan long trips because they are not sure the life is right for them.

Not all cruisers plan exactly what their cruising life will be until it actually happens. When she started cruising ten years ago, Barbara Marrett, a contributing editor to *Cruising World*, viewed cruising as a way to adventure off to exotic places. "I didn't expect it to be a lifestyle, but I really enjoyed it much more than I could have imagined. It's not having a set schedule; it's being very open, embracing the unknown, and letting your life flow instead of directing it."

How we cruise, where we sail, and the distance we travel varies, but the common threads between all cruising lives are adventure, freedom, challenge, and change. Whether you do it for the rest of your life or for one year at a time, you will grow and learn more about yourself and the world if you give cruising a chance.

Why We Go

I asked women cruisers why they went cruising, and I heard a variety of reasons for starting the adventure. When we begin, we all have our own individual reasons for cruising. After time, however, the women I spoke with seemed to share a similar commitment to cruising because of the opportunities it creates for travel, adventure, and independence.

"We went because of the adventure," said Lura Francis, an artist who shared the cruising dream with her husband Jack. "Our whole married life had been going to concerts, going to the city, civic light opera, galleries, taking a picnic lunch and watching the boats on the bay. We used to say that someday maybe we would get a boat and go."

Many people dream about cruising; only some are fortunate that their dream can become a reality. Lura and Jack waited for the opportunity to fulfill their dream, sharing a cruising life after they raised their family and retired.

Other women have cruised most of their adult lives. For them, cruising was not a future dream: It simply was life as they lived it. Lin Pardey was twenty years old when she started cruising. "I saw freedom in the life, unrestricted travel, and being free of material things," she says.

Now, thirty years later, Lin talks about having a homebase. (Long-term cruisers have a hard time using the word "house" when they talk about living on land.) "We will probably spend more time in our homebase when we get older, but I can't picture putting away the boat and not going again. Maybe we'd build a little boat again, so we could manage. . . . We know people still cruising in their eighties."

A slide show led to Patience Wales's desire to cruise. "We wanted to get out of our lives and into different lives. So we saved all our money for six years, made our own beer, sold our houses, bought our boat, which was really too big for us because we didn't know what we were doing, and took off. I think I went, more than any other thing, for the adventure. It is like no other kind of traveling. That was in 1964. I was young and foolish. Now I'm old and foolish."

In the process of building their fourth boat in 1995, some of her feelings changed. Now, Patience says, "I'm more blasé. I think I'm pickier. I know I'm less willing to be uncomfortable. But [cruising] really doesn't mean anything different from what it did the first time around."

I know many women who go along as a cruising mate. Paula Dinius said of her husband, "Dana was the real ramrod behind the whole thing. Because he was in a stressful position, for him it was a major escape. He dragged me through in the beginning, because I didn't have the passion he did. When we left, I was excited. I was excited about the adventure, but I was afraid of being on a boat at sea."

A first-time experience at anything can be daunting. Barbara Colborn, who is new to bluewater cruising, talked to me immediately after returning from her first ocean voyage. "I wasn't sure that I wanted to cruise for the rest of my life, and we agreed on trying it for a year. Reading books is one thing, but actually being out there and experiencing it is another."

The beginnings of any experience are key to its outcome. But few of us can predict in the beginning what shape our cruising lives will take. I did not grow up sailing and did not see cruising as a lifetime dream—or even a short-term goal. Jim and I bought our boat as partners, figuring the financial obligation we shared was sufficient commitment to each other. We had lived on board for less than a year when I discovered, after reading a news article, that our boat was scheduled for the Transpacific Yacht Race to Hawaii. I exploded at Jim for not consulting me, and then we made a pact. If the passage to Hawaii was not a good experience for me, Jim would buy out my half of the boat when we arrived in Honolulu. When we reached the Ala Wai dock, I announced, "I'm keeping my half."

That same summer the Australians won the America's Cup. We thought it would be a lark to sail to Australia to see the next competition, and so we went.

The two years we allotted for the voyage grew into a seven-year circumnavigation. Before we left we were married at the urging of family and friends, who worried about me traveling in countries where my rights as an unmarried woman might be in jeopardy. Sixteen years later, there is no doubt in my mind that sailing all over the world is the most exciting thing I can do with the rest of my life.

Demands and Rewards

"The best times I've ever had in my life have been cruising; also, the most uncomfortable times I've ever had have been cruising," said Barbara Marrett. She tells potential cruisers that cruising can be both the best of times and the worst of times; she was warned before her first passage ". . . not to expect a picnic. Experiencing ocean swells in a small boat can be very uncomfortable and frightening at times. So when I was miserable the first three days out, I was somewhat mentally prepared. . . . But the difficulty of sailing to the Galapagos and then Easter Island, our first landfalls, was repaid by the reward of exploring these incredible islands. I don't regret any part of the adventure, including the edge of the hurricane we passed through."

An early cruising lesson for me was learning to live with things that I cannot change. When Mother Nature has a bad day, I have to share it. Choppy seas, too much wind, not enough wind, heat, cold, heavy fog, broiling sunshine, and salty spray all have to be reckoned with at some time. Not only was it essential for me to learn to adapt to the conditions: I had to acquire the grace to accept them.

A young man crewed with us for several thousand miles. One day we were becalmed within sight of our port, and our engine was not working. In frustration, he shook his fists and hollered like a child having a temper tantrum. When I questioned his behavior he said, "I have never felt so helpless."

I was unsympathetic at the moment, but I also have days when things do not work out the way I want. But the bonus, most cruisers discover, is that Mother Nature has many more good days than bad days. Those good days are our reward for enduring the bad ones.

Adjusting to cruising can take time. Barbara Colborn reminded me of some advice commonly given to new cruisers. She said, "People who have gone cruising said to give it at least a year, and I found that it was true. Five months into it, I was still uncomfortable about some things and wishing to be home now and then."

Several experienced cruisers have offered wise words about aspirations. The desire to take on a big trip easily fuels your enthusiasm and imagination, but sometimes is not very realistic. Some people start out on a circumnavigation or a major passage and then discover it is not what they expected.

Migael Scherer offers advice to such cruisers. "Move slowly," she advises, "bite your trip into small chunks and do everything you can to build your confidence in yourself and your boat. Don't be afraid to turn back. There is no shame in turning back, and you should never regret it. Take those small steps first."

I believe if you feel insecure or unprepared for something, there is nothing wrong with rethinking your plans. Bad weather, inadequate navigation information, or boat-system failures can cause problems; those are the times to turn back to a safe harbor. Pride pushes people to do stupid things. Remember that there are no records at stake when you go cruising. The goal is your own enjoyment and satisfaction.

Cruising has its demands, but the rewards are many: exotic locations, adventure, excitement. For me, other rewards are the friends I have made along the way and the opportunities I've had to see history firsthand. Being a part of the natural world has also strengthened my belief in myself.

For Barbara Colborn, it took only a short time for her to see the rewards. When she was concluding her first cruising experience, she told me, ". . . we've been out fourteen months and two passages, to Hawaii and back. I love it and I wish I didn't have to go back onto land and earn money. But I think it was important to say, 'Okay, we're going to try this for a certain period of time and see.'"

For Nancy Payson, one reward is spending time in new places. "[My husband] gets me to sail because I like to get to places and be there for a while. The sailing isn't the reason most women go. Certainly not initially. If they're lucky, they learn to love sailing."

For Lura Francis, cruising was a way to grow and learn. It was "a life where you have time to think, experience solitude, know yourself and your partner, grow together. It was being resourceful, finding out how to do everything from changing oil to making yogurt."

For me there is another reward that I did not anticipate. One day my husband said, "Cruising wouldn't be any fun if I didn't have you to share it with." Then he told me that the worst thing he could imagine—worse than sickness or losing the boat—would be not being able to remember all that we had experienced together.

I realized our partnership is very special. Maybe I could have had that relationship without cruising, but it is unlikely anyone will ever convince me of that. The roles cruising partners share may always be changing, but the commitment to the relationship is never in doubt.

2

His Dream, Her Dream, Too

A LARGE MAJORITY OF CRUISING women sail with men. Whether they are married or not, the onboard relationship is critical to the success of the cruising experience. After interviewing cruising women about their relationships with the men they sail with, it was clear that there is no single formula for success. There are certain elements, however, that are common to good onboard relationships.

The Raison d'Etre

Most people dream about cruising before they turn the fantasy into a reality. When a couple shares the cruising dream, it is important that each has his or her own reasons for taking on the adventure. As Nancy Payson wisely advises, "Be sure you're doing it for yourself and not your husband, because you can get a lot out of [cruising] if you look at it this way. If you're going to be a martyr—and do it even though you want to keep the house or you don't think you'll like it—don't go."

We all have found ourselves the victims of self-fulfilling prophecies. We don't think we will like something, and sure enough, we don't. Nancy Payson cautions against prejudging: "I think women don't understand that you can enjoy yourself. You can get a big thrill out of all these things. You can learn and not be scared."

Migael Scherer understands that your motivation for cruising may not be exactly the same as your partner's, but says, "Your reasons need to intersect to have a successful relationship and a successful cruise." In her experience, building their 50-foot ketch together from the keel up was a binding force in her relationship. "We learned to work together from the beginning. We had the same goal: getting the boat built. We still have some disagreement, but it's part of the teamwork."

Although Lael Morgan and her partner divorced after their cruise, she has a positive attitude about their experience. "Cruising was a dream for both of us right off the bat. Our chemistry worked. I loved the dream, the idea of doing it. That kept us together. It was far better than anything I could have imagined."

Cruising Roles and Relationships

We purchased our boat before we got married. I paid half and shared the upkeep. I came into the relationship having skippered my own boat for several years as well as racing with my husband. There were many things I did not know about boats and sailing, but one thing I did know was that I did not enter into our boat ownership as a first mate: We were partners.

I know from experience, however, that there can only be one captain at a time on any boat. Whether you are cruising or racing, one person has to be ultimately responsible. Especially in emergency situations, there is no time for a consensus.

Since my husband has more sailing experience and skill than I do, he is the captain of our boat. We change our "titles" to suit certain situations. In foreign countries, we are listed as co-captains (or captain and pilot) to ensure equal status. I am the watch-captain when we have a crew, and I am captain in my husband's absence. I refuse to be called the first mate. This has nothing to do with the tasks I perform — it has to do with my own perception of my role. I view myself as a partner and always have seen our relationship that way. In some ways that has made my transition to sailor easier than it might be for some women.

As captain, my husband is in charge of the boat, but I question decisions or plans if I believe there is good reason. If I think we need to reef because the boat is heeling too much, we usually reef. If sailing conditions are poor for a designated departure date, my husband typically defers to my preference for delaying a start. He is not being macho and I am not being a wimp: My husband's tolerance for heavy weather, or his desire to move to a new port, causes him to look at the weather and other factors from a different point of view than mine.

Occasionally when I suggest a change, my husband points out a good reason why things should remain as they are. If, for example, I want to reef the mainsail, he may point out to me that the boat will be under-powered, and sailing will be more uncomfortable with reduced power in our sails. In those situations, we jointly assess the situation and determine the best course of action.

An emergency is never the time to challenge the captain or question his or her decisions. If I want an explanation, there is always time later to review our actions. If I see or hear something during an emergency that my husband misses, however, I offer the information, and he uses it in assessing the situation.

Despite the fact that no one calls me "first mate" more than once, I have taken on many of the traditional female tasks on the boat: cooking, provisioning, and bookkeeping. As my husband enjoys pointing out, I also am the manager, administrator, and chief executive officer. We could not go cruising if I did not handle those jobs.

My husband and I defined roles that work for us, and we function well with this relationship because we both can be what we want to be.

It is important to understand the roles you and your cruising partner will play. Many times those roles will follow the pattern you have already set on land. Women who have maintained a traditional role over a long period of time may find it difficult to change that pattern once they go sailing. If your husband or partner has been the leader in deter-mining your course for the future, you may not want that to change.

Migael Scherer explains that while she takes on responsibility for the domestic chores, such as cooking and laundry, she has expecta-tions about that role. "You need to make demands to meet your responsibilities. Food is the most important thing." If you do domestic duties on a boat, you are no less important than the person who handles the mechanical or deckhand duties.

Traditional roles work well for some cruising couples; others look beyond the traditional norms to learn what will work best in their cruis-ing life. Lin Pardey, an experienced and competent sailor, understands how traditional roles develop. "We all fall into some traditional roles. The biggest fear is he may not know seamanship so you must back him up or take charge as needed."

Novice cruiser Barbara Colborn expected that her husband, not she, would be captain. But, as she says, "As I learned more about weather and gained the confidence that comes with experience, we came to more equal footing."

Professional skipper Patricia Miller knows that, in order to ensure the safety of a vessel, a woman needs to know how to be in charge. Patricia's first cruising relationship was not a happy one. Her partner ". . . did not know much more about [cruising] than I did, but he had to be the captain. . . . He became a yeller. He'd never let me learn. He'd just scream and yell." Now, cruising with John Rains, she has a happier relationship that suits her and ensures better safety for their vessel. "Most women grow up being conditioned to function as part of a team, and that's perfect. But for safety's sake, a husband/wife cruising team needs to rotate captain duties regularly, at least on a practice basis."

Patience Wales believes that taking on responsibility is the only way to really enjoy cruising. "Women are too dependent on the men they are sailing with. I feel very strongly about that. I've seen it over and over. Invariably [what] it comes down to [is that] she feels she is only an adjunct. She's an arm or a leg. She's not in any sense the main body or even a body that can support his."

For cruising men, the ability to trust a female cruising partner is crucial. Without trust, there is a weak link in the relationship. British cruiser Gail Amesbury makes the point very clear. "The male attitude to the female on the boat is one of the biggest problems. If it's not right, that's when [the relationship] won't work. A man should lie down in the bunk and ask himself, 'Can I lie here for forty-eight hours and trust her?' If the answer is no, then he should wait until the answer is yes."

Taking on responsibilities can translate into pride and joy. "It's no fun to go along for the ride," Patience Wales says. "You should somehow be an important part of the crew. And if women would just understand that being in charge of something is fun, choose what they are going to do, and learn to do it well, that's the kick of it."

Communication Required

Many recent books and articles have focused on the different communication styles of men and women. Recognizing that there are differences can be a key factor in making the cruising partnership work.

Pat Nolan has taught men and women to sail, and she has watched how communication styles affect the way men and women function on a boat.

"Men communicate differently," she says. "They catch onto things in a different way. Men do things spur of the moment and don't do up-front talking about it. It causes problems because if no one knows what the job is, it ends with screaming and yelling." Couples sailing for a mooring buoy, for example, need to know who is doing what. They need to talk ahead of time, Pat advises. "That is the major difference: Let's talk about it. Women love to do it and men don't. [Men] assume you will know what they are thinking without telling you."

You may not agree with Pat's view of male and female communication differences and how they manifest themselves on a boat. But it is important to accept that there can be differences in communication styles. Be prepared to deal with them.

In her book, *Cape Horn: One Man's Dream, One Woman's Nightmare*, Réanne Hemingway-Douglass describes how she struggled to keep communication open to maintain her family relationships—especially difficult with a combined family. Looking back on the voyage, she says, "If we had had some counseling as a family, it would have made it easier for him to accept where I was coming from and how he handled the teenagers." They did have counseling when they returned. Réanne and her husband have continued to work on their relationship, and they cruise together every summer.

Misunderstood communication is common for cruising couples. You may find a given statement demeaning, or you may make a statement that is perceived as silly or unfair. Holding a grudge and allowing communication to become difficult puts your relationship in jeopardy.

Paula Dinius describes how she and her husband handle communication on board when feelings are on edge and sensibilities are raw. "We have a rule that things said on the boat don't count. If something is said that one of us can't forget, you have to take a shower, eat a meal, and take a nap before you can bring up what the other person said."

Seasoned cruisers recognize that sailing offshore creates certain stresses. Being clean, rested, and fed soothes your nerve endings and may change your perspective on a given situation.

Living the Dream

Good cruising relationships evolve over time.

Many cruising women have a situation similar to Nancy Payson's. "I deferred to him when we first started because he knew a lot more about it than I did," she says. "Now we are more [like] partners. He still has more strength than I do. He navigates because I don't like to. Our roles have evolved and we stick to them; they're comfortable."

Retired cruiser Lura Francis remembers how she and her husband Jack always functioned as a team. "We respected and trusted each other. He never put me down and I likewise for him. We [once] saw a couple anchoring and could hear the man screaming at the poor wife.

Jack said, 'We aren't going to do that.' We developed hand signals. It takes lots of preparation and lots of work to be a team."

Because you depend on each other and are always together, cruising can cause a certain intensity for couples. In one way, cruising is an opportunity for couples: It is a way of life where you need to become a team and build trust and respect. Cruising can also be the test of a relationship. Many cruising women agree that a strong relationship on shore will remain strong at sea. A frail relationship is likely to fail.

For Nancy Jewhurst, who sails with husband Vic and their son Kyle, cruising allows couples to spend a lot of time together when most couples on land seem to go separate ways. "He's out there with Little League. He has his hobbies, and the woman has hers. . . . In a cruising world, you have far fewer distractions, and it's a fairly intense life, which can be tough. But who knows how long we're here on this earth. I want to make the moments count. I think cruising moments count more than other moments."

Personal disputes that develop during cruising are often cited as reasons for divorce. Lael Morgan, who divorced from her husband after their cruise, believes cruising actually added to the longevity of her marriage. "I sailed with him later, and we are still good friends," she says. "We are both loners and we lived separate lives."

For me, the trust and respect I enjoy in my relationship are earned commodities. My time, effort, and perseverance have paid off many times over. The bonus was when my husband told me that the worst thing he could imagine was not having me out there with him to share our cruising experiences. We share good stories, scary memories, and private moments that are ours alone. It doesn't matter who had the dream in the first place. It only matters that, together, we made the dream our reality.

3

Getting Started

W HEN WE TAKE ON A NEW ACTIVITY, we formulate a list of questions in an attempt to visualize what will happen. This chapter answers frequently asked questions about learning to sail and being on the water. You may already have your own list of questions, and not all of them may be answered here. The answers to the questions in this chapter may increase your comfort level and resolve your doubts. Some of these topics will resurface in more detail in later chapters.

If you are not a sailor, it is likely that the first question on your list is, How do I learn to sail?

When I started cruising, I was surprised that some women were accompanying their husbands or boyfriends on cruises without knowing how to sail. As one woman cruiser told me, "I went along; I'm not a sailor. I went along all those years with the kids. I don't think I'm capable of taking charge of the boat." There always were others on board during passages, so she never felt in jeopardy. When there are more than two people on the boat, responsibilities tend to be shared. But I believe having several people share the responsibilities on a boat can contribute to a false sense of security.

As Barbara Marrett says of her first cruise, "I trusted John and his skill. I remember on our way out of the Straits of Juan de Fuca thinking, What would I do if there was a fire? What about a dismasting? I hadn't thought about certain emergencies until we were on the way out. I was involved with selling my business, saying goodbye to my friends. They had occupied my mind more than sailing had. I wished I had taken more sailing lessons and had spent some time singlehanding the boat." Barbara found a way to put her mind at ease: "I listed the emergencies I was concerned about and wrote down how we would handle them. I posted these instructions on a bulkhead near the radio so that in an emergency I could glance at the list as a reminder. Although we never had to use it, it gave me peace of mind."

With growing sailing experience and confidence in yourself, you lay the groundwork for successful cruising. Dawn Riley put it very simply: "I don't think anyone should be expected to feel comfortable and enjoy cruising if they don't know how to sail."

Where Do I Learn?

I am a believer in encouraging women to sail together, particularly to race together. I learned to sail without the benefit of a formal school. My first sailing experiences with my first husband were terrifying, and I grew to hate our 22-foot boat. I didn't learn well from him because I had no idea what the end result was supposed to be. In my first lesson, he told me, "Sail the boat around that buoy!" I didn't know how.

After finally gaining some understanding of how to sail our boat, I was able to follow my first husband's instructions. But I was always intimidated by him and the boat, and I had no desire to take the helm or to be skipper.

Over a year later, we bought a 26-foot boat. At that time, my husband decided to spend time racing offshore on another boat. Our boat sat unused until a friend asked me if I would participate in a women's race. I pointed out that I didn't even know how to get the boat out of the berth, let alone sail it. She said, "We'll learn."

We got a crew together, pieced together what little we knew, and sailed in the race. We didn't hit anything or anyone. We were so exhilarated that we talked about racing the boat against men. Interestingly, we were encouraged by everyone we talked to.

There were six women on the boat, all of whom were married to or dating sailors. We decided not to ask boyfriends or husbands to teach us to sail, since other women had had bad experiences sailing with their partners. So we looked for instructors. The only men allowed on board were several instructors, who taught us specific skills.

Our instructors quickly discovered that we were serious students not afraid to ask questions. The interaction among the women on board made it easy to handle mistakes and keep our enthusiasm high. We did not become the season champions, but we had a good time.

As the skipper, I had to learn everything. Besides being on the helm during the races, I had to take care of the boat, lift and operate the outboard engine, and make lunch. It was great experience.

Think about the best way for you to learn, for you have several choices. Sail with your mate as your instructor; attend a sailing school, or find someone else to teach you, and then go back and sail with your partner. You also can learn on your own.

Your Mate as Your Instructor

If your husband or boyfriend teaches you how to sail, I believe you should be responsible for the program. Specify what you want to learn and in what areas you need to build your confidence.

Start by drawing up a list of things you want to know (see my list of basic skills later in this chapter). Your list may be very general in the beginning, but you can make it more specific as you learn. The important thing is to ask questions until you hear the answer you are looking for.

Sometimes a question is answered correctly, but the answer may not give you the information you really want. In one of our seminars, a woman asked, "What do I do when it is windy and the boat is heeling over too much?" She was told to let off the mainsheet, which is a way to reduce your heel. But from her facial expression, I could tell this answer did not tell her what she wanted to know. She wanted to know about more than the simple mechanics of heeling: She wanted to know what you do when there is too much wind and too much heel, and you feel insecure about not knowing what will happen next.

Asking questions of a spouse or a male friend teaching you to sail may intensify inherent problems in communication. If the question is about a specific procedure, the answer is specific. When you are looking for a whole body of knowledge, you need to ask a lot of questions.

Pat Nolan has witnessed the different ways men and women learn on a boat. "Women want to know what the procedures are going to be," she explains. "They want to know what is expected so they can process [the information] and be ready." Pat believes more people today are aware that men and women communicate differently, and women are becoming more assertive. "Instead of saying 'Okay honey, whatever you say,'" Pat explains, "it's 'Hang on, let's talk about this.'"

Sailing in certain directions feels more comfortable than others. Being comfortable means feeling secure. This is the time to ask, What makes sailing in some directions more comfortable than others? If you're told, "Reaching and running are always more comfortable than beating," ask for an explanation. When are you reaching, running, and beating? Why does the wind seem different on these different points of sail? You'll have to understand these kinds of distinctions in order to control your environment better and make sailing a comfortable experience.

Each time you encounter something you don't understand, ask very specific questions. Your mate will quickly see that knowing how to control your environment is vital to your sense of security and comfort.

Not all of us are willing to learn from our mates in this way. If you try learning from your mate and the only result is frustration on both your parts, don't give up. Look for other ways to learn.

Sailing Schools

Sailing schools with professional instructors are a great way to learn, either by yourself or with your partner.

Taking lessons with your spouse may eliminate many potential problems. As Gail Amesbury says, "We learned side by side, starting at night school doing basic courses. It was a huge advantage. Neither one of us knew more than the other, and we relied on each other."

Lael Morgan, thirty years after cruising from New England to Alaska, agrees. "Take courses together so you know what is involved. Most women don't have a clue about the danger, the difficulty, and the work [sailing] is." To add to her point, if you learn together, you are not in the situation of wondering how much the other person knows.

If you are a beginner sailing with an experienced partner, it's likely your partner will not want to take lessons. Be prepared to go out on your own and find a sailing school where you can learn the basics. Most prospective cruising women have jobs, families, and responsibilities. Finding the time and energy to learn how to sail will take a conscious effort, but rest assured that your effort will help you get more joy out of cruising.

You can start educating yourself while looking for the right school. One of the most important steps is to learn the correct names for boat parts and maneuvers. Begin that process on your own. If you have trouble remembering different parts of the boat, put labels on them. Learning the language of sailing is the first step to equalizing your relationship.

Womanship developed the holistic concept of learning comprehensive cruising skills on board, rather than isolating specific skills to be taught one by one. Founder Suzanne Pogell describes this as "an accessible learning framework for women, who like the big picture of what they are aiming for." Suzanne's approach, format, and curriculum have been adopted by several schools that now specialize in teaching women. Among them are Women for Sail, Sea Sense, and Sistership. These companies have received good press in a variety of publications.

Pat Nolan, who has taught for Womanship and now owns Sistership, describes the philosophy of women learning together with women instructors. "When women sail with all women, they are more likely to express their concerns, their fears, their lack of experience. Women are very open with each other about their needs. They tend not to be so much so when there are men in the group: They don't want to appear inexperienced or fearful in front of guys. Women are more likely to jump in and try something new in an all-women atmosphere."

Women-only schools offer basic instruction in sailing, docking, anchoring, checking engines, and navigation. In most courses, the school's emphasis is not to turn you into a member of an America's Cup crew. Instructors begin with basic skills and move to more advanced skills as the students are ready. A student's level of confidence at the end of the course often is the program's measure of success.

Suzanne Pogell of Womanship explains her philosophy: "Women often tell us they lack the confidence to feel comfortable as a cruising partner. Our mission is to help each student become the sailor she wants to be, in her own way and at her own pace, in a practical sequence of steps designed to provide her with the skills, knowledge, and experience she knows she can depend on. This is the foundation of confidence." Suzanne feels that a woman's tendency to feel confident only when she knows she can rely on her skills is a positive attribute — one that should be acknowledged by both the learner and her partner.

These schools offer courses extending from two days to a couple of weeks on board 30- to 45-foot cruising boats. Some courses are half-days and weekends. In others, students and instructors live on board, sailing together for a week or longer. Classes are available for beginners, intermediates, and the ready-to-drop-out-because-my-captain-yells-at-me students. (The motto at Womanship is "Nobody Yells.") Programs are offered throughout the year in locations around the world.

"I took a basic sailing course and then a liveaboard cruising class from Womanship," attests Gail Bowdish. "It was one of the most significant things in my life. I came home with a lot of confidence in handling the boat and it worked for my self-esteem. I could take control over my life." Gail's reaction to a women's school is fairly typical.

There are alternatives to learning in a women-only school. The U.S. Sailing Association, the national governing body for the sport of sailing, put together a program called the Keelboat Certification Program in concert with commercial sailing schools. The program is appropriate for adults who want to learn to sail keelboats at all levels, whether you want to daysail or make offshore passages. US Sailing publishes a list of the schools that participate in the program. They also publish *Where to Sail*, a comprehensive guide to sailing schools, sailing programs, and sailboat rental operations throughout the country.

A program at a national sailing school might be beyond your budget or require more time than you can give, so it is important to shop around before you commit yourself. In my estimation, in a small group or in a one-on-one teaching situation, a week of half-day lessons will be enough for you to learn the basics. Talk to recent alumna of the school you're considering to get opinions and recommendations.

Learning on Your Own

If attending a formal program at a national sailing school doesn't fit your lifestyle or your budget, you can piece together an independent program of instruction.

Some well-known cruisers learned to sail on their own. Lin Pardey remembers her first sailing experiences as true hands-on trials. "Larry launched me in a dinghy," Lin remembers, "and then hollered, 'Lin, don't jibe; Lin, don't jibe; Lin, duck!' And I learned to sail." Patience Wales's experience was similar. She started sailing on a 12½-foot Herreshoff. After that, she says, "We learned as we went. We went down the Intracoastal. We had all the books, and we talked with a lot of people. We made a lot of mistakes and screwed up a lot. But we never screwed up permanently or in a way that was damaging to either the boat or ourselves."

Look for opportunities to sail on your own or on boats where beginners are welcome. One popular way to learn is to find one or two women who sail and are willing to take you along. If you wander down marina docks on weekends, you might come across a woman skipper who needs an extra crew for the day. In the process, you might even find a sailing mentor who improves her own sailing ability by helping you learn.

Some regional sailing magazines and newsletters have annual crew signups where potential crew are matched up with boats and skippers. These opportunities often are open to beginners. One word of caution: Make sure you don't sign up with a crew looking for someone who is decorative and good at opening beers. You won't learn much about sailing.

Check classified directories for marinas, sailing clubs, and boat rental operations. These operations frequently offer optional instruction where you can work out your own schedule and ask for instruction as you need it. Your local community college and universities may also offer courses in sailing that are open to the general public.

An excellent way to gain an overall picture of boating is by taking a course through the U.S. Coast Guard Auxiliary or the U.S. Power Squadron. These classes are taught by experienced volunteers, and they provide basic information on boat handling, nomenclature, boat operation, and regulations. The courses are taught locally and typically are free.

Both Lin Pardey and Patience Wales learned to sail on small boats when they were in their twenties. Even if you ultimately plan to cruise on a big boat, learning to sail on a small boat—such as a Sunfish, Laser, or Cal 20—equips you with basic sailing skills.

Nancy Payson cruised with husband and children for seven years on a larger boat before getting the opportunity to learn on a small boat. "The boys really wouldn't let me do very much, and I became the cook," Nancy says of her early cruising days on large boats. "I didn't learn as much as you think one would. Then we did a trailer [sailor trip] for a year-and-a-half. I learned more on that 22-foot boat than [I did on] the big one, and I learned more on that boat because of the reaction time."

Several years after I began sailing, I started sailing a dinghy. The mistakes I had been making on a bigger boat suddenly were magnified, because the small Laser dingy had just one reaction to the things I did wrong: It capsized. After spending some time in the cold water, I learned to pay much closer attention to wind direction and sail trim. As Barbara Marrett says, "I think it is a good idea to learn to sail on your own in a small boat before trying to pilot an expensive, intimidating cruising boat on the ocean."

Offering another perspective, Suzanne Pogell says that she learned and became comfortable sailing on a 36-foot Freres racer. "By the time I sailed an 18-foot boat, I loved its maneuverability and pulling those little strings, but if I had started out on a small boat, so close to the water, I would have sat rigid with fear. In our experience [at Womanship], adult learners prefer learning on a bigger boat and, when comfortable with their skills, to singlehand or share sailing a small boat."

Working knowledge of the mechanical and electrical systems on a large cruising boat is part of cruising skills. You won't gain these skills on a small boat, but you can learn about these onboard systems after you learn basic sailing skills and spend some time on larger cruising boats. Seminars and short courses in diesel mechanics, electronics, safety at sea, and heavy weather sailing are valuable. They don't replace knowing how to sail, but they should be part of your cruising knowledge. Local clubs, boat shows, the U.S. Power Squadron, and the Coast Guard

Auxiliary offer educational opportunities in these areas. I recommend looking for programs with a woman instructor. She most likely will be in tune with your needs. Contact information on sailing schools and other programs can be found in the Appendix, page 160.

Do I Have to Become an Expert?

In every endeavor there are levels of competence. Learning to swim can mean everything from staying afloat to competing in the Olympics. And so it is with sailing: You do not need the skill required to earn a gold medal in the Olympics to get your boat from one place to the next. The goal is to learn how to manage your boat.

What Do I Need to Learn?

When you are comfortable taking the helm and piloting your boat, you are on your way. From that point, the degree of competence you acquire as a sailor is your decision.

Learning to sail alone is critical to your survival. You may plan never to sail alone, but a time may come when you may have to. If you never learned to pilot your boat alone, your response could be panic. But if you know you can sail alone, your underlying confidence will make the difference.

For your own survival and peace of mind, as well as your partner's, I recommend being able to do the following without assistance or direction:

1. hoist and lower or furl the sails;
2. trim the sails correctly for the course you want;
3. steer the boat accurately on a compass course and on an apparent wind course;
4. turn your boat by tacking and jibing;
5. recognize what point of sail you are on;
6. understand the difference between apparent wind and true wind;
7. know when and how to reduce sail;
8. start the engine, drive the boat under power, and dock or anchor;
9. pump water out of the bilge;
10. check your engine oil;
11. plot a compass course and navigate from a chart;
12. use a sextant and do celestial navigation;
13. use your electronic navigation devices.

The reason for developing your own skills is clear. It will enable you to sail the boat if someone falls in the water. All good sailing schools teach recovery—the important thing is, can *you* do it? If you are alone because your sailing partner fell overboard, you need to bring the boat back to him and get him on board. There are techniques and equipment designed specifically for this type of rescue. Your security and peace of mind will depend on knowing how to use that equipment.

The mechanical and electrical systems on a cruising boat are integral to life on board. I strongly recommend that you learn the basics of those systems. To assume all women are not mechanically inclined is old-fashioned. You drive a car, thread a sewing machine, operate a computer, or parallel-park a car. All these tasks require some degree of mechanical skill. You might prefer not to do mechanical things, but I don't believe women are inherently unable to learn the mechanical tasks basic to a boat.

Even if you won't be responsible for these systems all of the time, be sure you learn to purge a line, check dip sticks, and charge batteries and monitor their condition. On some boats, partners share tasks equally—each changes oil, replaces pumps, cleans filters, shops, cooks, and washes dishes.

Your ability to do a job without direction is important, and confidence in your ability to do so will be your biggest asset. It will allow you to understand that your environment is not out of your control.

If My Partner Falls Overboard, How Do I Rescue Him?

Prevention is the key to avoiding falling overboard. Wearing a harness with tethers fastened to the boat will keep you both from falling overboard. Insist they be worn. If your partner is not wearing a harness and falls overboard, the first thing to do is deploy liferings and other flotation devices he can hold onto while you sail the boat back to him and get him on board.

In my opinion, the best rescue equipment available is the Lifesling, a combination helicopter lifting sling and floating horseshoe. The basic procedure is to tow the Lifesling behind the boat and position the boat so your partner can reach the device. Once he has the Lifesling in his grasp, stop the boat and pull the Lifesling to the boat (don't tow the Lifesling while the person is wearing it) and follow the manufacturer's instructions for hoisting him aboard.

There are many aspects to executing a proper man-overboard procedure. It is important you and your partner understand this procedure and practice rescues together. You will need to be confident about your ability to rescue a man overboard. Take advantage of safety demonstrations and courses.

How Can I Go Cruising When I Always Get Seasick?

Seasickness has several causes. Unless yours is caused by an inner ear malfunction, which affects your equilibrium, there is a good chance you can overcome seasickness.

Worry and fear frequently manifest themselves in the symptoms of seasickness. Overcoming fear by gaining experience and skill can help.

The most common form of seasickness occurs when your body is adapting to being at sea. Daysailing and weekend trips may not give your body enough time to make that adjustment. With time, your body learns a new set of perceptions and reactions so you won't suffer from seasickness. After many years of sailing, there are still times when I get seasick after being ashore for several weeks or living in a marina for an extended period of time. My body needs to relearn responses that have been unused for some time. See Chapter 7 for more on seasickness.

How Do I Keep the Boat from Heeling?

A boat moves because wind puts pressure on the sails. That pressure makes the boat lean or heel. A small amount of heel is normal in efficient sailing; up to twenty-five degrees is comfortable and efficient for most boats. To make the boat heel less, it is necessary to reduce the wind pressure on the sails. For example, you can achieve this by releasing the sheets (lines fastened to the free corner of the sail) so the sail "spills" some of the wind pressure. On certain points of sail, such as when you are sailing downwind and the wind is pushing your boat from behind, your boat will heel less and feel more comfortable.

How Do You Live in Such a Confined Space?

Comparing the living space in a house to the space on a boat certainly makes a boat seem confined. Reducing your possessions, both personal and practical, will simplify life and take up less space. A well-designed boat with good stowage and plenty of light does not feel confined to me. But a feeling of confinement is not just physical—it has to do with attitude.

Living in close quarters, twenty-four hours a day, means learning to respect each other's need for quiet and privacy. Minor annoyances must be dealt with so they don't become major issues. The cubic yardage of your boat will never be adequate without a give-and-take attitude and mutual respect.

How Do You Manage the Boat on Long Voyages?

The organization you impose at sea is called a watch system. For day trips you may not use a watch system, but as you progress to days of consecutive sailing and overnight passages, a watch system becomes essential.

When you devise a watch system, you and your partner divide the day up into blocks of time. You each will be responsible for one block of time, alternating watches so when one person is on watch the other person can rest. You can divide the day into three-hour watches, four-hour watches, or in any configuration that suits you. It's a good idea to consider who likes to stay up late and who likes to get up early when devising your watch system. See Chapter 14 for more information on watch systems.

What Scares You Most About Voyaging?

What scares me most is not being prepared for all the things that could happen on a voyage. In the past, ignorance has been the prime factor in my being scared. With each passage, I find preparation is still the most important ingredient in making me comfortable. The boat needs to be provisioned, and all systems need to be in running order. The route, with alternatives in the event of bad weather, needs to be discussed and agreed upon. An overall picture of the passage, including how long it will take and what to expect in terms of weather and sailing conditions, is essential for me. I don't have a crystal ball, but it's on my wish list.

How Many Storms Have You Encountered at Sea?

Fewer than I have living on land! We plan our route using pilot charts (charts of average weather trends for a given geographical area) so we are sailing to places where the weather is pleasant and the water is warm. We have encountered bad weather, including huge seas and winds in excess of sixty-five knots that once lasted about three days. It was uncomfortable, and I was frightened. Once we were in those conditions, my husband made it clear that we would just have to keep going. His advice sounded so simple and sensible: I just concentrated on getting through the weather. Looking back, I realize that was my only option. I trusted the boat to see me through.

How Often Do You Go Home?

Our budget is very limited, so we rarely visit the States. On a seven-year circumnavigation, I went back once for two weeks for medical treatment, and my husband and I went back together for five days when our youngest daughter got married. The travel cost, combined with the cost of leaving the boat, is expensive for us. You may have more options. Most of our family and many friends come to visit and sail with us for several weeks at a time.

4

A Boat
for Just
the Two of Us

SELECTING THE RIGHT BOAT is a major factor in determining how happy you will be cruising.

There is plenty of room for different opinions on what length your boat should be. But the most important thing to keep in mind when selecting a boat is that you are choosing for "just the two of us."

Cruising families and couples who share a boat with others may have different requirements and resources because their permanent crew numbers more than two people. But if you plan to sail the majority of the time as a couple, your boat should be customized for the two of you and where you plan to sail. You need to be able to manage your vessel and live with it.

We met a couple who had cruised for twelve years on a Catalina 27. They kept the boat on a trailer in Mexico and drove there from their home in Arizona to go cruising. They planned to retire and were trying to decide what their next boat would be. The husband was looking at bigger boats in the mid-30-foot range. But the wife was happy with what they had. "Let's keep this boat because it's easy to sail. We know it and we like it," she said. Few cruising couples today would consider a 27-foot boat adequate. But for some types of cruising, this size is perfect.

A cruising boat may be a small "pocket cruiser" suitable for one person or a trailerable boat sailed on weekends and vacation. It may be a fiberglass production boat turned out like a car from a factory or custom built of wood, steel, or aluminum. A cruising boat may be just about any kind of vessel you set out in, and there are many designs built for a wide variety of purposes.

I sail on a 48-foot, cold-molded wooden sloop built in 1970 for ocean racing. We bought *Nalu IV* in 1981 to live aboard and (as I discovered later) to race. When we decided to go cruising, we saw no reason to consider another boat. We liked and trusted the boat we had, and it was paid for. Originally raced with a crew of eight, *Nalu IV* can be sailed by two people, and by one person in an emergency. But we often have friends or family along because the boat is big and has few automated features.

Lin Pardey has been cruising for more than thirty years on boats under thirty feet. Her boat is built of wood and does not have an engine. It sails easily in all conditions. It is missing some of the amenities you might expect to find on board, such as a freezer or a watermaker, but Lin has other luxuries on her boat, including velvet upholstery and fine china and crystal.

When it comes to length, Lin uses a very practical approach to selecting the right size: "The kind of boat you want is one you can sail home alone without help because your mate had a heart attack." This reasoning may sound ominous, but it is based on excellent judgment. The possibility of your sailing partner being disabled or lost is always a reality, even when sailing close to home.

Patience Wales's taste in boats has changed over the years. Her first boat was heavy and slow with kerosene lamps and a wooden hull that required painting and scraping. The second boat was a Cal 39. It had no refrigerator, so they had to haul ice on board, and it didn't have an anchor windlass, so they had to raise and lower the anchor manually without the mechanical advantage of a windlass. On the third boat, they had to furl the sails, varnish the toerail, and set up awnings. The fourth boat, which she and her husband and another couple are building, will be over 50 feet with an enclosed deck saloon, in-mast furling so the mainsail will roll up easily inside the mast, lots of fresh hot water, AC power for all kinds of devices, and powered winches.

Patience describes her feelings as she moves toward the building of the fourth boat. "Being able to stand cold night watches in our snug raised saloon will be wonderful, but its very comfort amounts to a loss," she says. "We are giving up some of the challenges of sailing—the sting of salt, the shock of wet and cold. But most of all, we want to extend our cruising years. This boat seems to be carrying us in that direction."

The boat you select may be like the boats Lin, Patience, or I cruise on. Or it may be totally different. Use every opportunity to sail on different boats before you invest in one. You may be surprised at what appeals to you. In the end, choose carefully. The right boat can make cruising wonderful. The wrong boat can make it hell.

The Right Boat

Finding the right cruising boat takes time, and you need to invest enough time and energy looking at boats to learn what you want, what you need, and what you can live with.

If you live near a marina or a waterfront where boats are kept, start prowling the docks. Ask boat owners questions about their boat and how it suits the kinds of sailing they do. Most owners love to talk about their boats, and many will give curious folks a tour.

A boatyard, where boats are stored in the off-season and maintenance work is done, is also a great place to see what is involved in owning a boat, learn what problems boats develop, and study hull and keel shapes. If you have seen an advertisement for a certain boat, a boatyard is a likely place to see that boat's underbody and any visible problems that have developed below the waterline.

Visiting a boat show is fun and should be part of your research, but, generally speaking, a boat show is not where you will ultimately buy a boat.

Photos, stories, and advertisements in boating magazines will acquaint you with all types of cruising boats. Many magazines have classified sections listing boats for sale, with sellers' telephone numbers. Call them to talk about boats and costs.

Sailing on charterboats can be good cruising practice, but the boats in large charter fleets are not necessarily examples of good designs for long-term cruisers. Charterboats are designed for short-term sailing. They are crammed with amenities and maintained by someone else. Check small charter fleets, which may have a variety of boat designs from different manufacturers.

We tell our seminar participants that trying out a boat is essential. When you buy a boat—even a new one—it should be subject to a marine survey and a test sail. A test sail is not motoring around for an hour—it means going out and using all the sails in the inventory, with the engine off, to see how the boat handles. If there isn't enough wind when you go out, reschedule.

Another strategy is to find the type of boat you're interested in and get acquainted with someone who owns the same design. Find a boat that needs crew for a passage or a boat that is going to be raced. One couple took our advice one step further. They decided they were interested in a Valiant 40 because it was affordable, had a good interior layout, and was American built. They found three Valiants that were racing to Hawaii, and they called the owners to find out if they needed extra crew to sail the boats home after the race. They found a ride, spent nearly three weeks sailing a Valiant 40 in all types of ocean conditions, and ultimately bought a Valiant 40. They are happy with their choice, and there have been no surprises since they know the design well.

A Personal Choice

The right cruising boat ultimately is a personal choice, and we all have different qualities we want to find in a boat. I have outlined five basic points I use when looking at boats.

First, as a long-distance cruiser, you need to feel confident that your boat can take more than you can, which means sound construction. I want a used boat, because many construction faults develop in the first three years of a boat's life. I want a boat built and commissioned by sailors, not day-laborers who have no idea what the end product will be.

Second, the design must be a good sailing boat—not one driven by a marketing department trying to sell me upholstery or marble countertops. The sails must be reefable. I want a staysail, so I can have an extra sail for power or carry a small sail in bad weather. I want a tall rig, so I can carry big sails in light-air conditions. I prefer wheel steering that is operated by steering cables, because hydraulic steering has no "feel."

Third, the quality of life on board in all conditions must be as comfortable as possible. The boat must not roll. Bunks must be dry, able to hold me in place in rough conditions, and changed easily. The galley must be workable whether we are sailing upwind or downwind. The head must flush on either tack and should not require that valves be turned on and off each time. Every item on the boat must be stowable, from earrings to spare parts (even the captain, occasionally).

Fourth, routine maintenance and repair must be simple. Whether I am changing a halyard, washing dishes, or replacing a spreader light, I know that if maintenance isn't easy it won't get done. Varnished brightwork is gorgeous, but I don't want to spend every spare moment sanding. The cost of repairs has to be reasonable. Otherwise, I don't want the system—electronic or otherwise—on the boat.

Finally, I want a boat that is beautiful to look at. Boats that have a boxlike shape to create more interior space are ugly. A boat should look

College of the Ouachitas

graceful at anchor and underway. When someone asks me, "Which boat is yours?" I want to be able to say, "The pretty one."

Sailing Venue

Whether you sail in warm or cold climates is a factor in boat selection. A pilothouse is great for cold climates and wet weather. But the same pilothouse may have to be air conditioned in warm climates. Large, open cockpits make the perfect livingroom in the warm waters of the Caribbean or the South Pacific. But open cockpits are wet and cold in Alaska and the North Atlantic.

If you have been cruising farther and farther from home and find that your boat is comfortable and safe, stay with the boat you have until you are certain you need a different boat. Buying a new boat is not a guarantee that you will have problem-free cruising. It will take time to get used to a new boat, resolve minor construction and system glitches, and feel secure with your new vessel.

Size

Overall size and interior space are important, but wide-open spaces and size just for the sake of size are not qualities you should look for in a boat. Cruisers have plied the oceans of the world in boats of all sizes. We have several friends who have circumnavigated in boats less than 30 feet long. I find 38 to 40 feet in length an ideal size for a cruising boat. A boat that size is usually big enough to be comfortable and small enough to be manageable. I have in mind specific designs, such as the old Cal 40 or a C&C 38.

Only two of the women I interviewed sailed in boats over 50 feet; over half the women sailed in boats under 40 feet.

Patience Wales sails with her husband and another couple, and they have cruised bigger boats because there were four adults sailing on board. Nancy Jewhurst and her husband and son cruise full time on a Traveler 32. Jack and Lura Francis, both fairly tall, circumnavigated on a Westsail 32. Irene Hampshire and her partner are raising two sons on a 33-foot boat. Lin Pardey's boat is under 30 feet, and Barbara Marrett cruised on a 31-foot boat.

Nancy Bischoff has sailed on a Tayana 37 with her six-foot, six-inch husband and two sons for ten years. They planned the boat around the family's needs when the boys were young, but the design still works for them today. Each boy has his own aft cabin, giving him privacy and room for his possessions. The parents enjoy their privacy in a forward cabin. Crammed between the fore and aft cabins are the head, main saloon, and galley. Both boys actively pursue music and perform at the drop of an anchor. Space is at a premium with drum set, keyboard, bass guitar, and amplifier on the boat—as well as school books, boogie boards, snorkel gear, and fishing tackle. They are a two-dinghy family, since the boys have an active social life.

Some women might find the amount of space on a boat too tight for their taste. But Nancy Bischoff finds the physical closeness of a cruising boat a unique plus, especially where children are involved. (When her youngest son sailed on our boat for two weeks, however, I told him to stow his gear in the forward cabin. Moments later he hollered, "Empty drawers! I've never seen empty drawers!")

Some sailors view size as a safety feature. Certainly, boats under twenty feet can seem tiny in big seas. But crew from aircraft carriers talk about being overwhelmed by big seas, so size may be more of a psychological factor than a safety one. Proper design and solid construction are the most important safety factors on your boat.

How Does It Sail?

Sailing will be your means of locomotion, and the sailing characteristics of a boat clearly are important.

Older designs—with full keels, short masts, and round bottoms—may be more traditional, but they are slow to respond. They go upwind slowly, don't crash into the seas, and ride an anchor beautifully. They are comfortable sailing off the wind but tend to roll when sailed directly downwind.

Newer designs with fin keels and flat bottoms are quick to respond and typically are quick sailing off the wind. Many designs of this type, however, pound if they go upwind too quickly in big seas.

Many cruising boats compensate for poor sailing characteristics with a large fuel capacity and big engines. This is a "chicken and egg" problem. Typically, the more fuel you carry, the heavier you are, and the harder it is to sail. Therefore, you will need more fuel because you may be spending more time motoring from port to port. Dependence on fuel limits how far you can sail and will tap your cruising budget.

Living Space

Life on a cruising boat has a basic irony. The comforts that work well at the dock often don't work at sea.

For example, wide-open spaces are fine at the dock. Underway, however, you need to travel through the boat and get a firm handhold every inch of the way. There are ways to add handholds and create visual space. Prioritize the features you want based on how you plan to use your boat.

Many new boats offer conveniences such as double beds you can walk around and front-opening refrigerators. At the dock, the boat doesn't rock so you don't have to worry about falling out of bed. A front-opening refrigerator also spills out the cold air each time you open the door, but when you're plugged into shore power at the dock you don't need to worry about conserving electricity.

Basic to your overall comfort below decks are the length and width of bunks, the height of work surfaces, the depth of the icebox, the placement of the head, and the size and number of lockers and adequacy of stowage.

Bunks

I find the ideal situation is having two separate sleeping areas: a comfortable double bunk and a workable pilot berth that you and your mate can share at sea.

You'll sleep in the double bunk at the dock or at anchor. It may be a forepeak arrangement, a double quarter berth, or an aft cabin. If there are only two people living on board the majority of the time, it may not be necessary to have a separate cabin. The pilot berth is a single bunk where you will sleep when at sea, regardless of the sea conditions. The berth should be built with high sides so its trough-like shape keeps you secure. A single quarter berth or a dinette berth with a lee cloth also serves as a good sea berth. Since you and your mate will be on opposite watches, only one sea berth is necessary.

The bunks need to be long enough so you can stretch out comfortably, be wide enough to accommodate your hip width, and have overhead clearance so you can roll over or get out easily. When you are considering a boat, climb into the bunks and stretch out. Note how easy or difficult it is to get in and out of them. Remember, you will spend lots of time in your bunk, and altering a berth is not easy to do.

The Galley

Depending on how tall you are, the height of countertops and overhead lockers in the galley can present a problem. Our boat, originally built for a tall man (6'4"), would have been totally unsatisfactory if I were shorter. Our refrigerator is top loading, and I can barely manage to reach items in the bottom of the box. When it's time to clean the refrigerator, we joke about who will hold whose ankles to reach the deep recesses.

The opposite situation is harder to manage. If you are tall, raising counters to a comfortable height requires major reconstruction. Or if you don't have sufficient headroom to stand upright when you work in the galley, that area quickly becomes a place to avoid.

The galley needs to be roomy enough to accommodate both you and your mate and functional both at anchor and underway. If you plan to make any kinds of passages, the stove should be gimballed (installed so that it swings on pins to maintain a level position as the boat heels). Items in the galley need to be easily reached, particularly if you are cooking while wearing a safety harness. For long-distance cruisers, propane stoves are the standard. Kerosene and clean alcohol are becoming harder to find in many countries. Diesel is great in cold climates, but it's too hot for the tropics. Microwaves and electric stoves are fine if you can generate electricity on board or plug into shore power at a dock. Compressed natural gas (CNG) is used on charter-boats. But if you plan to cook frequently on your own boat, it is costly and inefficient.

Top-loading refrigerators and iceboxes retain the cold better, keep contents from spilling out, and are more efficient than front-loading units. The ideal refrigerator has both a top-loading and a front-opening capacity so you can use one opening underway and the other at the dock. Freezers and refrigerators require electricity and may require repair. If you are going to be far from skilled refrigeration repair, an icebox may be easier to live with.

Pressurized water is a great convenience when electricity and water are readily available. For long-distance cruising, manual pumps conserve electricity and water. For ocean cruising, saltwater pumps in the galley and head will stretch your freshwater supply. I cook with a saltwater/fresh-water combination on long passages. We wash dishes and pans in salt water; we rinse tableware and metal pans with fresh water and everything else with salt water. This way, I don't use salt in my cooking.

The Head

On boats, the term *head* refers to the toilet and generally replaces the word "bathroom." It is hard to tell whether the location of the head is satisfactory when a boat is docked at a marina or stored in a cradle at a boatyard. When you take a boat on a test sail, using the head will quickly tell you whether it is going to be adequate.

Is the head accessible from the cockpit? The farther forward the head is, the less comfortable it will be at sea. Can you sit on it comfortably without falling off? Can you pump it (or flush it) according to the instructions? Is there enough room in the head for you to get in and out of foul-weather gear?

Many boats have showers as part of the head. If you have enough space and an ample water supply, showers are a nice convenience. Many cruisers in warm climates, however, find outside showers satisfactory. They bathe in salt water and use the shower for a final rinse. A frequently used shower below decks is subject to mold and mildew; you must have an excellent ventilation system. The shower should also have a separate bilge so shower water does not run into the common bilge. This runoff can create an odor, and hair in the runoff can clog your main bilge pump.

We have two heads on *Nalu IV*. Both are equipped with "Skipper" model heads manufactured by Wilcox Crittenden. These heads have been used continually for fifteen years, and I wouldn't change them for anything.

The best boat plumbing is expensive. But remember that women depend on having a functioning head on board.

Adequate Stowage

A boat's interior space is truly livable when there is adequate stowage. When you live on board full time, you find that everything needs a place to be stowed. At first glance, a boat may seem to have plenty of space. But that space can shrink dramatically, depending on where you plan to cruise and how long you plan to be on board.

Think about stowing enough food for a few months. Where will you put your wet foul-weather gear when you come off watch? Books, games, videos, and writing projects all need a place, as do sewing machines, spare parts, tools, bed and bath linens, and dirty clothes.

If you really like a boat, and it is one you own or one you are contemplating buying, check all the places designed for stowage and then think about what stowage you can create. Can you turn a spare bunk into lockers and shelves? Can you open up some liner space (fiberglass boats usually have an inner liner) to make more room for stowage? Can you add space on the insides of locker doors by adding cloth pockets or plastic boxes?

Boat Gear

When selecting boat gear, take into account men's and women's differences in physical characteristics. Women are more likely to have well developed lower body muscles, while men often have more developed upper body muscles. Training and conditioning can develop and improve muscle groups. But training may not be something you can do or want to do.

A man may be able to use arm and shoulder strength to turn a winch; a woman may find standing over the winch and using both hands is better for her. Winches located on the cabintop under the dodger will be hard for many women to operate. Relocate winches so they can be operated easily.

The size of the winch is important. If increasing a jib or halyard winch to the next size means that either partner can use it equally effectively, it makes sense to invest in a bigger winch. Increasing the mechanical ratio on the outhaul, mainsheet, and traveler, for example, will make both partners equally able to do the task.

Many cruising boats have furling sails that don't have to be stowed, eliminating the need to hoist, lower, and fold sails. However, many sailors prefer to have the option of switching to different sails. Remember, your sail inventory needs to be manageable, particularly for heavy weather. Both partners should be able to raise, lower, or trim the sails. Our storm staysail is made of heavy, eleven-ounce Dacron and measures barely ninety square feet; I can manage the sail in heavy weather without assistance.

One way some couples solve sail handling is to have a split rig boat: a schooner, yawl, or ketch. With two masts, there are more sails. Those sails can be smaller and still provide the same power as a sloop or cutter-rigged boat.

A boat is designed to sail carrying a certain quantity of sail area. If you use less than the design calls for, the boat's performance will be affected. Be sure your sail inventory will provide maximum power for your boat.

It is essential for cruising couples to have some type of self-steering system. If there are only two people on board and you have to hand steer the boat every minute of every day, you will be exhausted.

There are two types of self-steering systems available. Many cruisers install both aboard their boats.

Wind vanes are mechanical devices that steer your boat according to wind direction. The wind vane can be trimmed to keep the boat at a constant angle to the wind. On long ocean passages where prevailing winds vary little, the wind vane is a quiet, effective device.

Autopilots are electrical devices that steer to a compass course. Determine what direction you want to go, set the autopilot, and the pilot maintains your course. If the wind changes, you need to trim the sails.

Some automatic systems have a separate sensor that will respond if wind direction changes. However, the automatic system cannot work on both a compass and a wind sensor at the same time.

Your personal preferences, size of your boat, intended cruising grounds, and budget will all play a part in determining what systems you install. Be sure that you understand how to operate the systems and can do simple trouble shooting.

Safety Gear

Rescuing a person who falls overboard is extremely difficult. The first rule is to wear safety gear that will keep you on board. If you are alone on deck, wear a harness with a tether that fastens to the boat. When your partner is on deck alone, insist that he wear a harness at all times. If you are challenged, point out who would have to perform the rescue.

Many new types of harnesses are available. Find one that fits you comfortably and will not injure you if you fall. Chest harnesses are normally designed to fit men; be sure you try on any harness before you buy it. Note the length of the tether that comes with a harness. An eight-foot tether on a small boat may let you land in the water. You would be better off with a four- or five-foot tether.

The Lifesling is an essential item for all cruising couples. It was developed by the Seattle Sailing Foundation in 1984 and is manufactured by Port Supply. All royalties from the sale of the Lifesling are returned to the Foundation.

A new version of the Lifesling received U.S. Coast Guard approval in 1995. It is the only reliable, workable device on the market for short-handed rescue of a man overboard, and it is the only one that will allow a small person to rescue a bigger person. As good as the Lifesling is, it will not work unless you practice with it and both partners are confident in using it.

A simple factor in safety is freeboard (the distance from waterline to upper deck level). It is harder to rescue a person from the water if you have seven feet of freeboard compared to only four feet of freeboard. The high freeboard may make your interior space bigger. But, in my opinion, that extra space is not worth risking a difficult man-overboard rescue.

Every cruising boat should carry emergency equipment: an EPIRB, a flare gun, a life raft, man-overboard gear, and a radio.

The EPIRB is the emergency position-indicating radiobeacon. No one should cruise without it; it is imperative especially for ocean passages.

When you activate the EPIRB, it sends a signal to orbiting satellites, which relay the signal to land-based stations. Those stations notify the nearest rescue agency.

There's an innovation in EPIRBs known as type 406. It has two improvements over earlier models. First, the owner can register it with the manufacturer so that, if the EPIRB is activated, the signal alerts the rescuers to the type of boat, name of owners, and who to notify in an emergency. Secondly, the type 406's signal can be forwarded to a ground station without the satellite having the ground station in sight. This model is more expensive, but it may add to your sense of security.

Flare guns are used to signal other vessels when you need help or need to be located. Usually, boats carry two types of flares, both of which can be accommodated by the flare gun. The smoke flare is of short duration and is used for signaling. The parachute flare stays aloft and can be seen at a greater distance and for a longer period of time, necessary for rescue situations. Flares do deteriorate over time and should be checked for current dates before they're stowed for a long passage.

Life rafts are essential. Some cruisers believe their shore dinghy is sufficient. Others (even more foolishly, in my opinion) think that extra flotation in their boat makes it a substitute for a life raft. A life raft is only for emergencies, such as sinking or fire, that require abandoning the boat. It is stored in a canister or valise, on or near deck, and will inflate automatically when the emergency line is pulled. The life raft is designed to carry a specific number of people and to withstand crisis conditions. Most life rafts come with emergency gear stowed inside, but it is a good idea to bring a separate bag with essentials such as spare glasses, daily medications, and a handheld radio, among other things. (You can learn more about this by reading Tony Farrington's book *Rescue in the Pacific*.)

Radios are discussed in several places in this book, including Chapters 9 and 10. In emergencies, a hand-held VHF radio that broadcasts and receives only for line-of-sight distances is important for communicating with rescuers or fellow cruisers who might offer assistance. The SSB, or ham radio, can be used to call for help on emergency frequencies which are noted in radio manuals or on ham nets operating in your area. In life-threatening situations the term "mayday" is used to call for help. Other emergencies (illness, broken mast, etc.) are identified by the term "pan."

Safety gear on board is only of value if you know how to use it. Seek out demonstrations and learning opportunities.

Upkeep

All boats require upkeep, and you will spend money on your boat after you buy it. These expenditures include the costs of maintaining boat, gear, and equipment, and may include the costs of design modifications.

If you cruise close to home, maintaining your boat will likely be fairly simple. An annual haul-out to inspect it and paint the bottom can be a quick weekend job, if you have some experience. The size of your boat will also determine whether the annual haulout is a small expense or a formidable one. Most boatyards charge by the foot for haulouts and lay days (days your boat sits in a cradle).

If you cruise to distant ports, your annual haulout and inspection is even more critical. Hauling out in a foreign country to find potential problems and make small repairs may be inconvenient, but it beats having major problems with your boat and equipment once you are sailing offshore or in a port that does not have adequate facilities.

To keep your life as uncomplicated as possible, consider upkeep carefully when choosing a boat. Make sure that daily upkeep is simple, whether it is scrubbing decks, washing dishes, or cleaning the head. A complicated or difficult task is most often ignored. If you want to cruise in faraway places, learn to repair or do triage on all your boat's systems. Otherwise, you can spend months and many dollars on parts and repair.

Before you buy any boat, new or used, hire an independent marine surveyor to evaluate the boat's construction and gear. Insist on going through the boat with the surveyor, so you can ask questions and understand how he assesses the boat.

There are two national organizations of surveyors (see listings in the Appendix) that you can contact for names in your area. Your local boatyard is a good source for recommendations, because they know surveyors' specialties and who is the most thorough. Avoid using surveyors connected to boat brokerages and those who do not have a national affiliation.

In the excitement of buying a new or used boat—or changing the boat you have—remember that the ultimate purpose of a boat is to bring you joy, comfort, and security.

5

Fearing the Weather Ahead

THERE IS AN X-FACTOR in cruising that is unpredictable and uncontrollable: the weather. You can time your cruising route so you will be sailing in waters with low incidence of storms and hurricanes. But it is a mistake to assume that you will never encounter bad weather.

No matter how highly developed our equipment and skills, total accuracy in weather prediction eludes us. On *Nalu IV*, we were caught in the South Pacific between Bora Bora and American Samoa in a storm that was developing from a tropical depression to hurricane status. Our anemometer, which measures wind speed, registered sixty knots, and the needle was pegged as far as it would go. We had been in the storm for three days before it showed up on our weatherfax.

"What is the worst weather you've ever been in?" is the question I am asked most frequently by people planning to go cruising. I can recall those days vividly.

I remember the storm in the South Pacific that I mentioned earlier. I remember sailing upwind along the west coast of Australia for eighteen days in winds blowing from thirty-five to fifty-five knots; eating, sleeping, and living with the howling wind and sea made me exhausted and miserable. A severe thunderstorm in the Chesapeake Bay was the longest twenty minutes in my life.

In retrospect, I can describe those situations in detail only because I have been asked to recount them so often. And I realize that this question about the worst weather I've been in isn't a question about the weather at all. The question is about being afraid of bad weather.

Weren't You Scared?

I have been absolutely terrified on our boat. I have also been absolutely terrified on land. The part of me that is fearful is always with me, whether I'm driving on the freeway or sailing across an ocean.

Running aground, encountering storms, and falling overboard are things we, as cruisers, fear. We think about possible scenarios and consequences. But until we actually experience the unknown, it is out there for us to worry about and to fear. It is normal to fear the unknown, unfamiliar, or uncontrollable. They make us vulnerable.

If you haven't been caught in bad weather, you have a gap in your experience. You may learn by watching movies and reading books and scary magazine articles. Those images fill your mind, and your imagination works overtime. Now you have something to worry about, so you worry.

Listening to the questions women ask me about cruising has brought me to a conclusion: I am not the only woman with an advanced degree in worrying. Lin Pardey noted, "All women are worriers. We have expectations to live up to." Even if you haven't acknowledged it, your capacity for worry exists.

Have you ever worried about how you were going to look at a party? Do you find yourself worrying about joining a new group? Do you worry about a new computer program? Do you worry about what is going to be on sale when you get to the store? It's all right to worry about those things. Some things may be more important than others, but worrying is part of a basic planning process. You want to know how things are going to turn out before they happen, and you want to be prepared. So you fill up your brain with all the "what ifs."

In that process, you learn there are "what ifs" you can take care of. You can prepare for eventualities. Worry pushes you to learn about safety gear, how to reef sails, and how to read weatherfaxes. In the worrying process you make lists, read, and attempt to plan for every circumstance. Sailing in bad weather, managing a grounded boat, and sailing at night are things you can learn to do. But worry by itself, the kind that does not inspire you to learn how to better handle a potential situation, can be crippling.

Patience Wales describes how fear can play a role in survival. "I've been afraid hundreds of times. I was afraid of not knowing what to do. . . .

I still am [afraid] when I don't know what to do. More than anything else, that breaks down into feeling out of control. [But] the thing about fear that's encouraging is that you learn what to be afraid of when you're ocean cruising. . . . I think for cruising there's a kind of smugness as [we] get more and more experience that 'we know what to do.' You need to be particularly afraid of a complacency and a smugness, and the fact that your own experience is any assurance that you're not going to die."

Gathering Information

When you have made all the constructive preparations you can for a potential crisis, move on to the next project. Put your fears about bad weather on hold until you can collect more constructive information and experience. Going to seminars, looking at videos, and reading books about handling bad weather can be helpful.

In gathering information, Lin Pardey learned an important lesson early on: Discerning between good and bad information is important if you are going to manage fear. "I think fear is fed by radios, talking with inexperienced people, information coming from the outside," says Lin. "We had been cruising for three years and I had never been afraid, except of expectations. When we got to the Canal—watching boats come through, talking to everyone coming through, and talking to two couples who were novices—I nearly walked off the boat. My fear came from other people. Talking to other people scared me. I wasn't listening to Larry or looking at the boat."

Lin is absolutely right about knowing the difference between good and bad advice. I'm not sure there is a way to learn the difference, except through experience. One thing that is a waste of time for me is reading articles or seeing films designed to titillate my imagination. *Dead Calm,* a movie that was popular several years ago, was designed to scare and horrify. Any similarity to the realities of cruising and sailing was accidental, yet many people wanted to see the movie because it was about cruising. Stories without substance don't improve my learning. It is important to ask yourself, what did this person do that was right? Try to evaluate the value of an article, book, or film by looking for the author's biography at the end of the story or reading an editorial review.

Reading analyses of bad weather situations that have happened can be worthwhile. Two excellent books about actual storms are *"Fastnet, Force 10"* by John Rousmaniere (W.W. Norton & Co., 1980) and *Rescue in the Pacific* by Tony Farrington (International Marine, 1996). There are important lessons to be learned from the storms covered in these books.

Information that is thoughtful, precise, accurate, and—above all—true will help you learn more about the unknown. Avoid basing your judgments on information from unknown sources and war stories.

Learning to Cope

More than thirty years ago, Lael Morgan was caught in Hurricane Ginny off Cape May with her husband Dodge. "We were out in the cockpit for three days, not far enough off shore. We took everything down, put out a sea anchor. I went below. I couldn't function. I prepared to die. I was so pissed because I woke up and hadn't died. I went up into the cockpit, and [my husband] tied me in [so I wouldn't fall overboard] while he went below. I was mad and I had decided to lick it."

Confrontation is the ultimate response to fear, because you face the unknown and get acquainted. Lael's description of her fear being replaced by anger is not unusual, although no one would choose to be caught in a hurricane as a means of overcoming fear. Dawn Riley's attitude is, "The key is to be prepared. Think about it before it happens. The worst is to be an ostrich and just try to ignore the dangers."

Barbara Colborn remembers her first bad weather experience: "We had been close-hauled for several days. Each time a wave pounded the hull it felt like we were being hit by a medium-sized car. Everything was rattling inside, and the boat seemed on the edge of control. I put my head in a pillow and I just screamed. I cried. I prayed, and my husband prayed with me. He said, 'You just have to wait.' So I learned I had to wait." Although Barbara says that she has since been frightened on boats, prayer and experience helped her build a reservoir of confidence to overcome her fear.

Barbara now prefers to stay on deck, she says, "because I'm out in the open and the noises are not as bad on deck as they are below."

Going below deck is often a response to fear. We sometimes like to think that if we don't see something, it isn't there. But in my experience, below deck is the worst place to be if I'm afraid. I have no idea what is happening, so my imagination and the noises I hear combine to create dreadful scenarios in my mind. There is nothing more frightening to me.

Confront the unknown thing you fear. Don't give in to the urge to go below and hide. Snap your harness tether into a safe pad-eye and sit it out. When you have gained some confidence, adjust your tether so you can go forward and look at the rig, the sails, and the water. Steer the boat in this kind of weather.

Paula Dinius, who experienced the Queen's Birthday Storm, rode out some of the worst weather imaginable. Her faith in the integrity of her boat was paramount to overcoming her fear. "I was afraid of the power of the wind," she says. "After the hurricane, I am a lot less afraid . . . not that I think I can't die, but I trust the boat. . . . After all the things happen that you're afraid of, I'm confident that I [know] what I can do."

Advocating that you go out in a hurricane would be imprudent, and I am not suggesting that you risk your life in order to be happy cruising. Exercise the opportunity to confront the things you are afraid of and put them behind you. You need to know that your boat will take care of you, regardless of how you feel.

Sailing in strong wind is an opportunity to confront the weather and deal with it. An afternoon of "bad" weather may quickly become an afternoon of windy weather. If the wind blows above twenty knots, don't go home immediately. Keep sailing. The next step is to stay out when the wind kicks up more, maybe to thirty knots. If you sail on a sound boat with sails reefed and life jacket and safety harness on, you should be able to manage fine.

As Paula Dinius says, "By living with the boat over time, you get this bond and you get to know [the boat] and what it can do. That's what keeps me going farther and staying out longer: confidence in myself and my boat." She attributes her survival in June 1994 to knowing that her boat would take care of her and her injured husband.

Patricia Miller took a very pragmatic approach to her fears. "To conquer a small but lingering fear of drowning, I took a scuba class that taught me to navigate underwater in the open ocean. Now, whenever I'm frightened of the ocean, I spend a few minutes looking realistically at what would be the worst that could happen. After taking every action to stabilize the situation, I mentally rehearse what I'll do to survive it. After that, I just take deep slow breaths and observe the beauty, because in the midst of even the worst storm, there's dramatic beauty."

Learning all you can about the things you fear and how to cope with them allows you to exercise control over yourself and your environment. As Patricia Miller says, "If you allow fear to occupy your attention, it can paralyze you mentally and physically, thereby robbing you of your power and options. Sheer fear has never done anyone any good. But taking intelligent action on your own behalf will rescue you and evaporate fear at the same time."

Steering Clear of Bad Weather

There may be sophisticated electronic equipment that provides us with weather information, but it is unwise to put total faith in it. Elaborate, expensive gear and the best possible planning cannot protect you from encountering bad weather. Prepare for the weather and use common sense.

Pilot Charts, a Basic Tool

Part of your preparation is knowing when the prevailing winds are in your favor and knowing what times of the year you can expect storms and difficult sea conditions. Pilot charts can help in your planning. They do not give daily weather information, but they do tell what weather trends to expect for certain geographic areas.

Weather data has been collected over the years and is compiled on pilot charts. Information is grouped by regions: for example, charts are available for the South Pacific, the Indian Ocean, and the South Atlantic. For each area, there is a pilot chart for every month of the year, providing a summary of the average weather conditions. A system of symbols and codes details information about winds, wind direction, days of calm, prevailing currents, wave heights, iceberg intrusion, shipping lanes, tornadoes, and typhoons.

If, for example, you are trying to determine the best time to sail across the Atlantic Ocean from Europe to the Caribbean, the pilot chart for the Atlantic shows which months have hurricane-force winds, currents running in your favor, and winds blowing in a favorable direction.

We like pilot charts because we can visualize a passage, plan our stops, and get an overview of what to anticipate each month. We also carry *Ocean Passages for the World*, published by the Hydrographic Department of the British Navy. The volume summarizes the world's passages and ports traditionally used by sailing vessels. We rely on charts first, however, because books condense information we want to see in detail.

Daily weather information is available via weatherfax, WWV radio, and the studious use of a high-quality barometer. Some cruisers also use computers and satellite connections to receive weather information. But remember, there is no guarantee that the forecast is accurate.

When Paula Dinius advised land-based radio operators in New Zealand of the extremely high winds she was experiencing in the South Pacific, they found her report hard to believe: The weather did not coincide with the forecast. It was not until a rescue plane flew overhead and corroborated her findings that broadcasters believed her reports of the weather.

Use pilot charts for long-range cruise planning and purchase the charts that fit your cruising route. (Used pilot charts may be adequate, since information is averaged over many years.) Use onboard electronic weather equipment and learn to read the barometer.

What Do You Do to Prepare for Bad Weather?

Bad weather makes me crazy. I don't like wearing the same smelly clothes and not washing my hair. I hate being jammed into my bunk to sleep. I don't look forward to cleaning up after a seasick cat. After several days in the same soggy clothes, stiff salty hair, and moss-covered teeth, I am not nice. Who would be in those conditions? I look awful, feel frumpy, and would give anything to be anywhere but where I am (chances are my husband has similar feelings—even if he doesn't say so).

A positive way to deal with bad weather is to take control of the situation so that comfort, rather than fear, is the issue.

Equipment

You may use up your entire wardrobe trying to keep dry in a long stint of bad weather. If your clothing gets wet, change it. Keep your head and hands covered. Maintain body heat to delay the onset of fatigue and help prevent hypothermia. When you go below to eat or rest, strip off outer gear. In short: Take care of yourself.

Good foul-weather gear protects you from the elements. If you daysail or sail only on weekends, you shouldn't need to invest in expensive gear. But if you cruise long term or in severe weather, expect to pay several hundred dollars for gear that fits properly and keeps you dry.

At present, most good foul-weather gear is unisex, which really means it's designed for a man. A publication from the National Women's Sailing Association (NWSA), entitled *Women's Sailing Resource*, lists sources for gear designed for women.

When you invest in high-quality ocean-going gear, consider the overall weight of the clothing. My foul-weather gear weighs ten pounds and is exhausting to wear, but it keeps me dry and warm.

I wear a men's extra-small size for a good fit. Make sure that wrist, ankle, and neck openings can be made watertight. Some manufacturers incorporate nice features, such as fleece-lined pockets and high collars for cold weather. Be sure to find out if the company that manufactured your foul-weather gear will alter it if it does not fit properly.

Overalls under a foul-weather jacket may seem bulky and cumbersome but will protect you when worn without the jacket. And when you sit or bend, there is never a gap at the waist between your jacket and pants that can fill with water.

Try on foul-weather gear with the kind of clothing you intend to wear underneath. The right underlayers can mean the difference between comfort and misery. New synthetic fabrics have been developed to perform in cold, wet environments. For example, a fabric called Capilene wicks moisture away from the skin and insulates by trapping air in the fabric's interlocking knit.

Think about the gear you will wear on your head, hands, and feet. You will find waterproof seaboots, Synchilla hats, and gloves made out of neoprene and synthetic leatherlike fabrics in the wardrobes of cold-water sailors.

Boat shows are good places to research different kinds of gear, since many of the manufacturers and their representatives are in attendance. Ask other sailors what gear and what combinations of garments and fabrics work for them.

Everyone on board should wear harnesses and tethers during bad weather. There should be pad-eyes at the companionway so you can fasten your tether to the boat before entering the cockpit, and another at the steering station. Your tether should be no more than four feet long to ensure that you stay on the boat if you fall.

Discomfort

Preparation is essential for battling the discomfort the weather can cause. If there is no safe harbor close by, you need to get ready. Organize food that is easily prepared; shorten the watch system so you don't have to spend too long a time on the helm; maintain body heat with warm clothes, including hats and gloves; and drink as much water as you possibly can.

You must eat. You burn fuel rapidly in bad weather, and eating helps prevent fatigue. Hot food at least once a day will do a lot for your morale and your energy level. Even instant hot cereal or soup will taste like a real meal. If you have advance notice of bad weather, cook a pot of something that will keep in a pressure cooker on the stove. A pot of rice with anything thrown in for color and flavor makes a meal. It can be reheated without the pressure cap, and the sealed lid is handy in rough seas. Have a thermos of boiling water on hand for soup mixes, hot chocolate, or instant coffee.

Don't let concern about fat intake dictate your food intake. Frequent snacks of fruit, cookies, or trail-mix will help you. If you become nauseous in rough weather, try to manage some food intake — even if it's only crackers or dry biscuits.

Standing watch in bad weather requires being on the helm at least part of the time. Concentrating on steering in bad weather is exhausting. The normal three- or four-hour watch will be too long. Take shorter spells and periodically try to stand a longer watch so your partner gets some sound sleep.

I admit that I hate drinking lots of water during bad weather because getting undressed to use the toilet is a major Olympic event. A rolling boat, zippers, Velcro, and a head without a seat belt all conspire to bruise and batter you. But a full bladder is impossibly uncomfortable, so you have no choice. I tried one of the funnel devices designed to equip a woman like a man, but it was impractical: In bad weather, you don't have that many hands. Drinking water is my least favorite advice — but probably the most important. Dehydration can make you very sick and render you completely useless. Drink water often.

Practice

There are several techniques to employ when the weather gets bad. Reefing sails, heaving-to, and deploying sea anchors and drogues are skills that require practice to perform them with confidence when the time comes.

Reefing a sail means making the sail area smaller. Reefing sails reduces your power aloft, and smaller sails make a boat more manageable in high winds.

Many cruising boats have roller furling sails, a system that allows you to roll a sail up quickly. On our boat, we reef the mainsail and change to smaller headsails. We have never needed to remove our sails completely.

Heaving-to, putting your boat into a holding pattern at sea, is a technique frequently used in heavy weather. This procedure keeps the boat from making progress but allows you time to rest, eat, or make repairs.

Assuming you know how to heave-to without practice is a mistake. Learning before you are in a situation that demands heaving-to is part of your preparation. Each boat has its own peculiar characteristics determined by hull shape, keel, and sail plan. Learn how to heave-to in calmer conditions and gradually practice the technique in more wind and rougher water. Always maintain a watch when you are hove-to.

Drogues and sea anchors typically are used in very bad weather. Depending on the type of boat, drogues and sea anchors will be deployed from the stern or from the bow. Dragging drogues and sea anchors will slow your boat down if reducing your sail area hasn't sufficiently slowed your speed. Sometimes drogues are used to keep a boat with a steering failure on course.

On-the-water seminars, videos, and books explain the above techniques in detail. You should practice these procedures and develop the best procedures for your boat. Learning these techniques will allow you to control situations before they control you.

The Silver Lining

Bad weather does have its silver lining. There is nothing so glorious as the first bright morning after a storm when you peel off those stinking clothes, scrub your skin till it glows, gorge on every morsel you can hold in your stomach, and curl up in the sunshine for a nap. When we talk about weather, we can guarantee one thing: It will change. Bad weather fades quickly.

6

Pirates and Protection

ONE OF THE MAJOR ATTRACTIONS OF CRUISING is visiting exotic places. The opportunity to live in new places, participate in new cultures, and experience new lifestyles can be a heady experience. But the thrill of going to exotic places is often dampened by our fear of those same places, their people, and their practices.

Many Americans have a preoccupation with personal security that dominates their lives. For some, the preoccupation is gained from the media and its sensationalism of violence. For others, it is gained, unfortunately, through personal experience. Violence in an exotic setting can become front-page news. If there is a murder in the Caribbean or piracy in the Orient, the media has a new story with which to feed our national paranoia. As a result, we are as afraid of the rest of the world as we are of our own country.

There are some truly dangerous places around the world. There also are places with customs, practices, and poverty levels that we, as visitors, need to be aware of.

Isn't It Dangerous Out There?

I cannot speak for all cruisers. But based on my own experience, my answer is no, cruising is not dangerous. I feel safe on my boat and in foreign countries. At the same time, I have had encounters that could have been dangerous in different circumstances.

We were in the new fishing harbor at Melilla, a small Spanish enclave on the north coast of Morocco. Our boat was moored stern-to at the dock. We had been befriended by the local fishermen from Spain who had warned us that the "Moros," the local Moroccan population, were "bad." But they gave us no further details.

During the night, I woke up and went into the galley to get a drink of water. I heard a noise from the aft cabin and assumed it was my husband coming in search of water. When I turned back to our cabin, a small, dark, bearded man wearing a track suit stood at the foot of the companionway ladder. My first thought was to hit him, but I was holding a plastic liter bottle filled with water that would not hurt him in the least. My second thought was to yell loudly enough to wake my husband and our friends in the forepeak.

I hollered my husband's name at the top of my lungs. The little man threw his arms over his head and started shaking his head vigorously back and forth. My husband, barely awake, charged out of the bunk and fell head first, tripped by the bed sheets wrapped around his feet. The little man scampered up the ladder. My husband's body on the floor blocked me from pursuit, and—as we laughingly acknowledged later— our lack of clothing prevented us all from chasing the intruder.

I wasn't hurt. I was angry that someone had come aboard without permission. I felt the way a mother feels when she wants to punish a child for a breach of manners: The little man had run away before getting his due. Fortunately for me, his small size, his defensive stance, and the element of surprise made me feel in control of the situation. A few more inches or pounds on the intruder might have made all the difference in my reaction to the entire incident.

Your reaction to the unexpected can determine what may or may not be a dangerous situation.

I was frightened by local boats while we were anchored in Malaysian waters. A boat came alongside and tied a line to us. Soon another boat came along. We signaled that he wasn't welcome, but he tied up to the boat already tied to us. Within a half-hour, eight boats were strung behind us like cars in a train. Their crews were eating, mending nets, making preparations for sleep, and ignoring us completely. It dawned on us that we had anchored in a regular anchorage spot for the fishing fleet. Our anchor was already down, and they thought it was perfectly sensible to tie off their stern rather than put down their own anchor.

Our immediate response was fright, but as we watched the situation develop, we realized we were not in danger. Similar situations have escalated because cruisers reacted aggressively, sometimes with firearms.

Nancy Bischoff worried about being in Mexican waters when she and her husband left San Diego. "I was apprehensive," she says. "I haven't seen anything in Mexico that makes me nervous. I heard stories, but they didn't keep me from cruising. We had a panga [Mexican fishing boat] tie up to us while we were underway. They were drunk. They wanted cigarettes. We don't smoke, so they smiled and then took off. It could have turned out differently."

Hearing stories and rumors makes all of us nervous. "It makes you afraid. You feel like you always have to look over your shoulder," says one woman cruiser. "I was worried about going up the Red Sea. We don't carry a gun. We never had any problems."

We had planned to make a quick passage through the Straits of Malacca because of the pirate stories we had heard. Our intended six-day passage turned into a three-month stay. The stories of danger, like many tales told at sea, were embroidered beyond recognition. The story of a reported shooting, at least ten years old, kept surfacing in a manner that made it sound current. But we learned from cruisers who had recently sailed the Straits that no one had encountered any problems.

When you don't have a means to evaluate reports, you have to take them at face value. Some cruisers suggest that such stories keep the beautiful cruising grounds of Southeast Asia pristine and uncrowded.

There Are Some Real Dangers

Pirates are real in Southeast Asia, and the potential for danger does exist there. Large merchant vessels carry cash in their safes, since crew are paid in cash at the end of a voyage. These vessels are the targets of waterborne thieves, and the owners have learned that it is more prudent to allow robberies than resist the boardings. Word passes among the cruisers to avoid the areas where these thieves are known to operate.

But as one cruiser who has sailed many miles in the China Sea explained to us, pirates know they will find money on ships. Small cruising vessels are likely to yield nothing but angry owners and a fight. His opinion was that the pirates were smart enough to know the difference between "a fat hog and a wild cat."

Drug traffic is a source of problems for cruisers in Asia. Again, knowledge passed among cruisers says to avoid congregations of native boats or high-speed craft. If you attempt to anchor in a questionable area or approach a suspicious-looking group of boats, you are courting disaster.

Many potential cruisers have expressed concern about being hijacked by drug runners who want boats. Most of our information about boats being hijacked refers to high-speed boats that can outrun the authorities. Cruising boats generally don't fit that category.

Cruisers must also recognize danger ashore. Many countries cruisers visit have large numbers of extremely poor people. If you flaunt wealth in this environment, you can expect trouble.

Lael Morgan acknowledges the risks they took in the 1960s. "We were both gamblers. We were going to Haiti; they had just hung an American. People were so poor. We did go to Caracas expecting trouble. We were fired on and then discovered it was a welcoming salute."

Lin Pardey takes a no-nonsense approach to the issue of security. "We've visited sixty-seven countries and been in five hundred foreign ports, and never felt threatened in any case, except the Philippines. The military explained what to avoid and offered to provide an escort. Sometimes there are areas to avoid."

The United States is often seen as an unsafe place, and some foreign vessels choose not to cruise in U.S. waters. Migael Scherer presents a scary picture of our own country as a cruising ground. Migael has spent nearly all of her cruising years in Puget Sound. In her memoir, *Still Loved by the Sun*, published by Simon & Schuster, she describes recovering from a rape at knifepoint. The incident occurred in broad daylight in a locale familiar to cruisers: a laundromat.

Her feelings of security changed dramatically. "There are jerks on the water like [there are] jerks on land. . . . You can be in a harbor and there's theft. We lock the dinghy to the boat. We lock the hatch when we go to sleep; we lock ourselves in. At anchor, we don't assume we're invulnerable. People think they are invulnerable. I think women have fewer experiences of being in control, and the experience of having [control] taken [away] leaves you powerless. You fear the world."

Still, Migael has not been deterred from cruising. "I, and numerous women who have had my experience, learn to overcome such fear and continue to seek out adventure, just as fear of storms doesn't prevent joy in cruising."

How Do We Protect Ourselves?

Concern about crime is legitimate in America. Based on the experiences of most cruisers, the rest of the world doesn't necessarily have the same problem. Still, I believe you should develop good habits from the outset.

Traveling in Company

Flotilla cruising is popular, but it needs to be organized carefully. Irene Hampshire found herself in the middle of a bad situation created by other cruisers. "We got into a group of American cruisers and sailed with them," she says. "We probably should have gotten out, but we didn't. It seemed all right." Her family ended up witnessing a fellow American in their flotilla needlessly murder two fishermen. It took the joy out of cruising in Mexico for her, her husband, and her two sons.

Although cruising in company with other boats can offer a sense of security, it turned into a bad experience for Irene — one she will always remember as part of cruising.

If you are sailing in company, it is crucial for you to know and trust the crew on your buddy boat. According to Dawn Riley, "We were in the Bahamas doing an overnight passage and a large, suspicious-looking fishing trawler approached us. I was on the bow, and they held the boat with grappling hooks and asked for cigarettes. We told them we didn't smoke, but they kept near. Fortunately we were cruising with another boat and called them over the VHF [radio], stating loudly that we were being approached and asked them to answer and flash their masthead light on and off. The trawler must have heard because they immediately took off into the night. Traveling with another boat is always a good idea."

Carrying Weapons

On our first long-term cruise, friends concerned about our welfare pressed us to carry weapons on board. We took a handgun and a shotgun. We declared the guns upon arrival in each country and were faced with turning them over to officials, locking them aboard the vessel, or storing them off the boat. Carrying weapons into a foreign country created such problems and paperwork that now we refuse to carry them. Not everyone shares our feelings about firearms, although many agree.

Patricia Miller learned to use a sling-shot while she was cruising solo in Mexico. "Now my husband often keeps a small gun handy at night."

Lin Pardey's reaction to having weapons on board was shared by most of the women I spoke with. "In the rest of world, guns are rarely used and it's safer," says Lin. "We don't carry weapons. We have had friends killed by their own weapons." A recent tragedy verifies this unfortunate fact. A boat in Panama was boarded by convicts. To protect himself, the captain produced a gun. He was disarmed and shot, ultimately dying from the wound.

A Canadian provincial police officer once told us, "In my country, only criminals carry guns." That is the perception, if not the truth, in many countries of the world. Of course, the United States is unique in protecting the constitutional right of citizens to bear arms.

If you decide weapons are necessary for your own security, know how to use them and carry them legally. Attempting to carry undeclared weapons has dire consequences in many countries.

Attention-Getting Goods Aboard

Another potential problem is liquor. Judicious use is one thing, but using alcohol as a trading good can create serious problems. In many Muslim countries, alcohol is illegal or extremely limited, and it is not uncommon for locals to ask for it. In remote villages in Mexico or the Caribbean, fishermen often ask for liquor as payment for shrimp and lobster. In some ports, officials even ask for whiskey as part of the check-in process. If your boat gains the reputation of being a "booze" boat, you can become a mark. Displaying other commodities of value, such as jewelry or cash, can increase your security risk.

Other Things You Can Do

Remember that as a cruiser—whether you are sailing in your local waters or far away from home—you are part of a community that enjoys traveling the world in a simple fashion without fanfare. Unlike the charterer who has a two-week vacation and doesn't have to live with the consequences of inappropriate behavior, your actions can follow you wherever you sail.

When we began cruising, we contacted the State Department for information on "hot spots" around the world (their hotline telephone number is 202-647-5225; website address is http://travel.state.gov). If there is political unrest in a place you want to visit, contact the country's embassy or consulate and talk with them about your plans. We have found that many places that have questionable reputations are wonderful cruising grounds.

Lin Pardey exercises caution to diminish her likelihood of being a target. "We take precautions. We lock the boat. We talk to people about the local area. We have a low-key-appearing boat and no rubber dinghy. We never had a theft, except a bailer from the dinghy. The important thing is to be low key."

Boat appearance can be a key to how you will be treated, but a low-key appearance doesn't mean looking neglected. A boat that doesn't show pride in ownership is as likely to be trashed as a fancy boat with lots of accessible toys. Some argue that appearing derelict is an invitation to being stripped of all gear. There certainly are rules about salvage that might justify that thinking.

Just as a boat bristling with antennas, fast tenders, and scuba and fishing gear may attract thieves, an inappropriately dressed cruiser is asking to be noticed. In the United States, we are used to dressing without regard for the opinion of others—particularly in large metropolitan areas. But, when cruising, your appearance and behavior can affect your reception and, subsequently, your security.

If you cruise away from home, I believe it's important to exercise restraint. A quick look ashore with binoculars or a glance in a guide book will show you how locals dress.

Using a phrase book allows you to use a few words of the local language, and it demonstrates that you have made an effort to learn about the culture.

Shopping with an appreciation for local food—instead of demanding peanut butter, frozen vegetables, and microwavable products—makes you a popular visitor rather than an unwelcome stranger. Put-downs of local products as inferior to American standards won't endear you to anyone and may make you a target.

Failing to recognize the local standard of living and practices is a frequent mistake. In the world's large cities, many styles, standards, and types of behavior are acceptable. It is easy to become absorbed into the local scene without calling attention to yourself. In a small town—in the United States, Europe, or the South Seas—your presence is obvious. A new boat in the harbor, a new face in the market, or a different language singles you out as a stranger. To me, it is obvious that wandering through the streets of a poor town wearing gold jewelry, flashy clothes, and carrying wads of cash is unwise. Yet cruisers forget to exercise common sense. The smart cruiser dresses neatly, carries minimal cash, and leaves the jewelry at home.

My Own Approach

Looking at my experiences and those of other cruisers has led me to devise my own approach to personal safety.

- I do not want guns aboard my boat, because they don't make me feel safe. And they can create problems in a foreign country.

- I am careful in my choice of companion vessels and friends on shore. Just because a vessel carries the same nationality as I do does not mean its crew shares my values or concerns.

- Stopping at a new port is an endeavor that requires advance preparation—including researching the standard of dress, the area's cultural and religious practices, and the local language.

- Carrying unnecessary money, wearing jewelry, and wandering unescorted in unknown neighborhoods or after dark is taboo.

- Trading liquor, ammunition, or drugs with locals is inviting disaster.

I am not willing to give up cruising, but neither am I willing to cower in overcrowded ports because of a fear of "bad guys," whether real or imagined. Common sense, intelligence, and some basic precautions go a long way in protecting your welfare as you visit the exotic ports of the world.

7

In Sickness and in Health

A CENTURY AGO, doctors prescribed an ocean voyage to cure many ailments. "The salt air will do you good," they said. If I were a doctor, I would offer that same prescription: cruising and salt air, on a regular basis.

Many people living in the fast-paced modern world seem unduly stressed—by jobs, family problems, and traffic, among other things. But when you meet cruisers, that harried expression is missing. Constantly looking at a watch, talking on the phone, and checking a daily appointment book are not what cruisers do. Cruisers are organized, but they are not harried.

Most long-term cruisers say they are the healthiest they have been in their lives. But that does not mean you won't have to make an effort to stay healthy and fit. As a cruiser, you have to take a more proactive approach toward managing your health. Gail Bowdish, M.D., offers sensible advice: "Make lifestyle changes in your diet, stop smoking, and reduce the risk for yourself. Understand the risks of cruising, acquire knowledge of what to do, take precautions, and work within your limitations."

Make preparations before you start cruising in terms of your own medical training and the medical supplies you carry on board. You and your mate will also need to get complete physical examinations before you leave—to better understand the status of your health and to take care of problems that can best be handled while you are still at home.

Medical Preparation and Planning

Planning to live without ready access to medical care requires forethought and training. In the United States, we are fortunate to have 911 emergency numbers, large hospitals, and well-qualified medical professionals. We assume that the rest of the world doesn't offer this same quality of care, which is not necessarily the case.

"Medical care is superior cost-wise in most countries, and extremely good," says Lin Pardey. She and her husband paid $310 for eye surgery in South Africa, which included all costs for doctors and the hospital.

In remote islands and Third World countries, finding a doctor can be difficult. So can finding someone who can speak your language in a medical emergency (a good phrase book should include a few basic phrases on doctors and emergencies). In those situations, you may have to be prepared to attend to your own medical needs. There are several ways to make health problems less worrisome while cruising.

Training

First, acquire some training. Courses in Advanced First Aid, First Responder Courses, and Emergency Medical Technician (EMT) programs offer varying degrees of preparedness. If you have the inclination, the 110 hours for the EMT program may be well worth your while. On the other hand, basic first aid, the Heimlich maneuver, and CPR may be all you choose to learn. Whatever level you aim for in training, spend time learning how to recognize basic problems and understanding what emergency treatments are required.

Some medical courses are designed specifically for cruisers. A woman who sailed with us had taken an EMT course and a medicine-at-sea course. In her opinion, the four-day cruising course, which was given on a boat, was more valuable. Local clubs and sailing magazines are your best resource for locating these courses.

We have two good medical books on board that are a permanent part of our library and dog-eared from use: *Where There Is No Doctor* by David Werner, published by The Hesperian Foundation of Palo Alto, California; and *Advanced First Aid Afloat* by Peter F. Eastman, published by Cornell Maritime Press.

David Werner's book is used by health care workers around the world and by travelers and people living in remote areas. It discusses symptoms and treatments and includes an excellent section called the Green Pages, which covers medications. Peter Eastman's book includes hands-on information for handling situations at sea. It has a recommended medical kit that can be easily modified for your situation.

I took an advanced first aid course to qualify our boat for an ocean race. My title for the race was Doc. I was not faced with anything more serious than constipation and a bruised knee, but the experience made me appreciate the need to be prepared when you go off-shore. I have always believed that if you are prepared for something, it won't happen.

I have learned how to give shots, close wounds, and remove fish hooks. At times I have been afraid I might hurt the patient, but reminding myself that not doing the required procedure was even more harmful was sufficient motivation to do what I had to.

Medical Kit

Your onboard medical kit may be anything from a basic prepackaged drugstore kit to a large duffel with many separate pouches, depending on where you go and for how long. The effectiveness of your medical kit also depends on your ability to use it.

I made ten small canvas bags with drawstring tops and labeled each one to cover certain medical situations. Among the labels are kits for common problems, medications, burns, major trauma, etc. The master inventory for each bag is posted in a plastic sleeve on the locker where the bags are stowed.

There are similar, prepackaged medical kits for cruising, with all items for specific problems in labeled zippered pouches, all of which are put into a large sea bag. Check sailing/cruising equipment directories for types and manufacturers of these kits.

Whatever you include in your medical kit, it must be packaged carefully—especially if you sail in a saltwater environment. Avoid ferrous metal zippers on kits; seal scalpel blades and scissors in plastic bags; use desiccants to reduce moisture and mildew; and be sure your prescription drugs are current and sealed.

We try to avoid daily rummaging in the first aid kit by making a few items readily available in the galley, including bandages, aspirin, and Super Glue (cyanoacrylate). The latter item is used for broken nails and quick sealing of cuts (but be sure not to let any glue seep into the wound), as well as inanimate object repair.

You can buy dental kits that a non-professional can use to mend broken teeth and lost fillings. New technology in epoxy makes repairs quick and semi-permanent. Many cruisers find a toothache the most excruciating pain possible. Pain killers are an essential part of your dental gear. Check sailing/cruising equipment directories for these kits or ask your own dentist to prepare one for you.

Drugs and medications are available without a prescription in many countries. If you need to take something regularly, such as prednisone, you may find it cheaper locally. This also will keep your supply current, rather than buying a supply at home that will last a couple of years. Antibiotics are readily available in many countries, so you will be able to keep an up-to-date supply on hand.

Many cruisers believe drugs should be kept in locked containers, but I believe emergency items must be readily available, and I have never been required at home or abroad to lock medications.

Medical Records

Before departing on a cruise, everyone should have a complete medical evaluation. A standard evaluation includes blood and urine tests, a Pap smear, and a mammogram. It is very important that you communicate to your physician where you are going and what you plan to do. Standard treatments and care may not fit your travel plans. Be sure your doctor understands the limitations in health care that you expect to face. In your round of medical visits, be sure to include stops at the optometrist and the dentist.

If you assume the responsibility for onboard medical care, be sure everyone on board provides up-to-date, accurate information, including medical records, prescriptions, test results, and X-rays. I encountered resistance from my husband when I suggested he get a physical exam. He stalled and told me he had one when he went into the army some thirty years earlier. Once convinced that I could not perform brain surgery or heart transplants at sea, he agreed that my request was reasonable.

If you wear glasses or contact lenses, take a copy of your prescription and extra sets of prescription glasses and contact lenses with you. If you wear contacts, be sure to take your glasses. Extended exposure to a saltwater environment may cause eye irritation for contact wearers. If you scuba dive or snorkel, a mask fitted with your eyeglass prescription is a nice addition. Life underwater is exciting when the curtain of fuzziness disappears.

The dentist can give you your most recent X-rays. If you have been postponing a crown or the pulling of a wisdom tooth, have it done before you leave. Waiting to reach a port to see a dentist is hard on you and everyone else aboard.

Cruising to distant countries may require a variety of immunizations. Check the requirements well in advance of departure. Current international health requirements are listed in the publication *Health Information for International Travel*, distributed by the U.S. Government Printing Office in Washington, D.C. (call 202-512-1800 to order).

The Centers for Disease Control (CDC) in Atlanta, Georgia, operates the International Travelers' Information Hotline (telephone 404-332-4559). Call to obtain information on immunization requirements and recommendations. The Hotline will tell you what disease risks apply to your itinerary, and they also have information about disease prevention. They have current information on, for example, sudden outbreaks of cholera. You'll have a choice of listening to recorded information, which can be quite long, or receiving the information by fax.

Shots and serums were formerly provided by public health agencies but increasingly this has become a private sector business. Check with clinics in your community.

Health Insurance

Your regular health insurance may cover you while you cruise. However, many cruisers have found that they won't be covered if they leave the country. If you need to secure new medical insurance before you go cruising, start looking early.

For trips of short duration, travel agencies may offer suggestions on programs typically used by vacationers. These programs, which cover emergencies and travel back to the United States for care, typically are short term with coverage limited from six to twelve months.

I have used carriers, such as Blue Cross Blue Shield, that offer catastrophic coverage. There is a high deductible, which essentially means you cover medical costs as you go. But if you're stricken with a major illness or emergency, the insurance covers you and, in many cases, requires you to return to the United States for care. If you are in good health, this may be the most economical insurance.

Foreign carriers provide health insurance useful to cruisers because coverage is not limited by duration of travel or the location of care. Two companies used extensively by long-term cruisers are listed in the Appendix. These companies have been known to pay claims quickly and are easily reached.

Private Patients Plan, in England, provides reasonable coverage once you leave the United States. Once you leave North America, insurance costs are generally fifty percent less than in private U.S. programs. If you come home for a visit, it is reported that the English company will not renew the insurance unless you leave within a three-month period. Make sure to check their policy.

International Health Insurance of Denmark offers a program that is similar in cost and covers you around the world. You have a choice of coverage, but there are cost limits that would not meet typical fees in the United States. This program offers coverage for individuals up to age seventy-five.

The availability and costs of insurance programs change constantly. Stay abreast of health insurance trends and information, some of which may be covered in sailing periodicals.

Many cruisers go without insurance and are comfortable with the risk. We currently use the Danish program and are quite satisfied with it. Your budget and health requirements will dictate the best course for you.

Help and Emergencies

As Gail Bowdish, M.D., says, "When it is a true emergency, sail to port and get an ambulance or the fastest transportation to the nearest hospital. Catastrophic events need medical care. These can happen anywhere."

The U.S. Coast Guard does respond to emergency calls if they are within reach. In other countries, obtaining assistance may depend on your ability to communicate your need and on available government services. Merchant vessels and military vessels may offer assistance in some situations. But remember that the reality of cruising is that there is no 911.

Some help is available by radio. A program called the Medical Advisory Systems Hotline or MASH (telephone 410-257-9504) is designed to help people who have medical problems when sailing offshore. For an annual fee, they assist you by phone, radio, or fax—wherever you are. A qualified caregiver is available twenty-four hours a day. You provide them with complete medical histories of the people on board, and they respond with a thorough questioning, discussion of your medical supplies, and a recommended treatment.

My one experience with this service was not in the case of an extreme illness. I contacted them when I had a reaction to a wasp sting. I was concerned about swelling and red lines extending up my arm. A calm voice on the other end of the radio assured me that they would stay in touch and monitor my condition. After two days of contact, during which I followed their advice, the swelling sub-sided and the lines disappeared. The best part was knowing that a knowledgeable professional was standing by with a sincere interest in my well-being.

Medical Concerns
Seasickness

Debate flourishes on seasickness. There are endless theories about its causes and cure. Bad weather (or worrying about it) can produce seasickness. Stress, worry, and fear can cause nausea, chills, and a range of symptoms typically associated with seasickness.

As Patience Wales said, "Feeling that I don't know what I should do physically, I get seasick. It's out of fear. I know that."

A small portion of the population gets seasick from disorders of the inner ear that affect the equilibrium. No drugs or techniques seem to work. I have great respect for people who suffer from this disorder and continue to sail.

The majority of victims overcome the symptoms of seasickness with remedies ranging from wrist bands that pinpoint certain pressure points to ginger and prescription drugs.

The anti-seasickness drugs I find most common are Marezine and Dramamine. Neither requires a prescription; both make the user sleepy and must be taken in advance of symptom onset. At present, many cruis-ers who suffer seasickness use Stugeron. It is popular because it is effec-tive *after* the onset of nausea. It is a prescription drug in the States, but it can be purchased over the counter in many foreign countries. The TransDerm ear patch, once popular because it alleviated seasickness without causing drowsiness, has been removed from the market in the States and most foreign countries due to undesirable side effects.

The first time I went boat shopping, I couldn't even go below decks on a boat tied at the dock. Even the gentle rocking motion, which is normal in any marina, sent me back on deck. Today, even if we have been in port for a time and then go out into rough weather, I know that I can't go below for six to eight hours. It takes that long to get my sea legs back. But if the weather is nice when we start out on a passage, going below presents no problem.

My workspace on the boat is a quarter berth that converts to a desk. It faces aft and allows me just enough room to work at the com-puter. In port or at anchor, the workspace is perfect. But when we are under sail, even after I have my sea legs, I can't sit down at the computer without developing the symptoms of seasickness in a matter of minutes. Instead, I sit on the sole next to the companionway ladder, facing forward, with the computer on my lap.

Your body needs to adjust to sea motion. Steering the boat, watching the horizon, and actively moving with the boat's motion are ways to get your sea legs. Going below and sleeping may solve the problem for some, but it can also prolong it.

Avoid reading or doing other close work. If you begin to yawn or experience chills or sudden warm spells, sit up on deck, watch the horizon, and breathe deeply. If you wait until your stomach is queasy, you may have passed the point of no return. It is not unusual to have the same symptoms on land when you return to shore after being out cruising.

The way a boat sails can also make you seasick. Rolling back and forth or yawing in light winds is worse for me than heavy weather. Some find that the pitching of a boat, the fore-and-aft motion, makes them sick. Sailing diagonally across the waves can reduce some of this up-and-down motion.

I don't take medication for seasickness because I need to get my sea legs in order to be comfortable, and medication postpones that adjustment for me. If you experience symptoms, don't give up. You need to find out what works for you.

Menstrual Cycle

Menstrual cycles, pregnancy, and menopause are issues common to all women. With increasing numbers of women sailing, questions about dealing with these life patterns are common. Generally, there is little difference in how you manage these events cruising or on shore.

Dawn Riley faced a rigorous life skippering a boat in the Whitbread Round-the-World Race. She dispatched of her period in a practical manner. "My solution was to take my [birth control] pills straight through. The doctor said that it was okay for a limited period of time."

Suppressing the menstrual period is an option many women choose if they are only concerned about a short period of time, such as a matter of months. Over the long term, the physical and emotional distress that many women experience has to be dealt with on a more permanent basis.

Premenstrual syndrome (PMS) is a problem many women face. The close quarters of a boat make it important to have the understanding of those around you. If a husband or boyfriend is aware and sympathetic, life is easier on board.

Barbara Colborn devised a way to communicate those times to her husband. "I learned to put a little lightning bolt on the calendar for the days I thought would be really bad. Some months were bad and I tended to be more nervous and on edge, more prone to some depression. But, it was no worse than on land."

What Barbara says may be the most reassuring thing a woman who suffers from PMS can hear: It was no worse when she was cruising.

"Menstrual cycles are never problematic," reports Patricia Miller. "I use tampons and I take vitamin B-6 whenever my hormones inflame my emotions."

A number of women ask about disposal of napkins or tampons. Unless you are using totally biodegradable brands (read the manufacturer's label), these products should not go overboard. If they are biodegradable, dispose of them only beyond the limits specified by local and international law. (The minimum under the MARPOL Treaty is at least twenty-five miles offshore and never in inland waters.) A double, self-sealing plastic bag will suffice for soiled supplies until you can reach a proper shoreside disposal.

There was a time when sanitary napkins and other supplies were hard to find. Unless you are going to be in very remote areas for an extended time, a six-month supply should be sufficient. Store supplies in sealed plastic bags or containers.

Pregnancy

In times past, it was suggested that women who were unhappy cruising could save face and go home by becoming pregnant. The pattern was to sell the boat, hop a plane, and have the baby at home. Today, pregnancy does not mean automatically giving up the cruising lifestyle. Some cruising couples look forward to having a family as they travel.

When we were in transit through the Suez Canal enroute to Cyprus, we befriended a couple expecting their first child. Their 24-foot boat had no engine, and they were towed through the canal alongside a sand barge. The trip on the Red Sea had been arduous. When she told me she was pregnant, I asked if she had seen a doctor. "Not yet. I'm only three months along," she replied.

She saw a doctor in Cyprus and continued to sail during the summer. Two weeks before she was due, she stopped at Malta and gave birth to her son. They completed their circumnavigation, bought a bigger boat, and set sail again.

As Gail Bowdish, M.D., says, "The risk of miscarriage is greatest in the first twelve weeks. Twenty-five percent of all pregnancies don't make it past the first trimester. It's a natural consequence and not all pregnancies are going to survive." In the early stages, she states, nutrition is important, and medical advice is important as the pregnancy progresses. "Contact with a doctor should be established," she says.

The risk of trauma increases during the second trimester. Pay attention to moving about on the boat, since falls are a cause of pregnancy loss. Because cruising is flexible, difficult or long passages should be avoided during this time.

"Premature labor can be caused by dehydration and stress," Gail points out. "Rest and drink plenty of fluids. Consider a shore-side residence approaching the third trimester," she suggests. A shore-side residence in the third trimester will also allow you to establish a relationship with a local physician.

Gail notes that a healthy woman should not be overly concerned about giving birth, especially if it is not her first pregnancy.

Every woman who is pregnant, whether on land or boat, understands the importance of proper medical care, nutrition and prenatal care, and knowing what activities pose risks to pregnancy. Cruising women who have children during their voyages have the same responsibilities as pregnant women on land. The main difference is that a cruising woman has to learn how to fit pregnancy into the unique circumstances of the cruising lifestyle.

Menopause

Many people begin cruising in their late forties and early fifties, the time women are most likely to enter menopause.

I received a letter from my sister filled with concern because I was not taking any hormones during menopause. To appease my conscience, I made an appointment with my doctor. After a lengthy discussion of the pros and cons, he told me he didn't want to prescribe hormones and have me head off to some unknown port where I couldn't stay in touch with him. With no family history of heart disease, cancer, or osteoporosis, I did without hormones.

I did have hot flashes as we sailed through the Southern Ocean, and I practically wore my clothes out taking them off and putting them on again. But there is no way of knowing if my life might have been easier had I taken hormones.

To stay informed and comfortable during menopause, talk with your doctor and other women and stay current on the use of hormones. For women who will be long-distance cruising, the reassurance of a discussion with a medical professional is invaluable. If you're making long-range cruising plans and are concerned about when menopause is likely to begin, remember that menopause onset is known to be similar among family members.

The major health problem related to menopause is the loss of calcium, leading to osteoporosis. Falling on a boat is dangerous if calcium is deficient. After menopause, a calcium supplement may prevent further bone loss, since your system is no longer able to make new bone. In early adulthood, you establish your calcium account by a good diet. Later, you draw the calcium from that account just as you draw funds from your retirement savings.

I take generic calcium tablets daily. Many calcium-rich foods are available around the world and are easily prepared on board. I eat a lot of yogurt, and I make fresh yogurt when we are underway. Beans, cheeses, and the ultra–heat treated (UHT) milk that comes in a box are all easily managed on a boat, even without refrigeration.

For some women, menopause and cruising mixed without aggravation. "I was always so busy saving up tampons, and suddenly I had a year's supply and I realized I was in menopause," Nancy Payson laughed, describing menopause as a non-event.

"I went through menopause without recognizing it," says Lin Pardey. "I am healthier now and I took hormonal therapy for a year to alleviate the most annoying problems. Pills were available everywhere."

Skin Protection

Both you and your partner are subject to serious skin problems when you go cruising. According to Gail Bowdish, the damage may have been done long before you took to the water. "Exposure as a child turns up decades later," she says. "The important lesson is to use sunscreen and protective clothing and avoid sunburn at all costs. The burn does the damage to your skin, and a severe burn is more likely to burn again."

I protect myself by using a sun shade and wearing lightweight cotton clothing to cover my arms and legs. In warm, tropical climates, I often wear long, loose, cotton dresses. A hat with a visor or brim and dark Polaroid sunglasses are part of my regular attire.

Many cruisers continuously exposed to the sun get basal cell cancers. These are not considered life-threatening but are aggravating and ugly. The cancer known as a melanoma, which can also develop on the skin, is extremely serious and can be fatal. Any unusual changes in your skin—from patches of dryness to blotchy pigment or tiny bumps—should be examined. If you have a history of keratosis, basal cell cancer, or melanoma, spend time with your dermatologist. Discuss your cruising plans and find out how to best protect yourself.

If you are determined to be a bronzed cruiser, you can choose from a wide range of products that both color and protect. Despite the fact that sun exposure has damaged my skin, I don't like to look pale. I use a combination cream that blocks the sun and colors my skin called Neutrogena Glow Sunless Tanning Lotion. When I get the desired color, I use moisturizers with sunblock.

Fitness

I am often asked, "How do you get exercise?" On a boat, space for jogging or even simple exercise equipment is precious or non-existent. "Plan for getting exercise, regular exercise, if you can't get enough on the boat," says Michelle Simon, M.D. An extremely athletic person may find it important to schedule off-the-boat exercise to maintain a normal level of fitness. For others, being on the boat may provide sufficient activity.

The normal motion of the boat and your body's continual effort to counterbalance those movements is around-the-clock exercise. Steering the boat or staying on your feet while cooking requires you to tense and relax your muscles as you synchronize with the boat's motion. Like isometric exercises, this activity goes on at a low level, even while you are asleep. If you have been sedentary, this much exercise will improve your fitness level.

Spend time trimming sails, grinding winches, hauling the anchor, and doing other cruising activities on board. The more you actively sail the boat, rather than use an automatic steering system, the more calories you burn. Sitting all day and reading a book while an electronic or mechanical device steers the boat deprives you of exercise and a chance to build your skills. You may not feel the exhaustion you feel in the gym or on the tennis court, but aggressively sailing the boat will help you maintain body weight and feel rejuvenated.

Yoga, even if you have never tried it, is excellent exercise on a boat. It helps you stretch and tone your body. It will also keep you limber and better prepared for quick movements or short bursts of intense activity. Almost anywhere you can stretch out will provide sufficient space.

Opportunities to maintain your fitness level exist in port, too. Provisioning a boat requires trips ashore. Rowing ashore is great exercise. Walking from shore to the store is very different from the weekly trip to the supermarket in the car. If you are in a country where open markets are the rule, shopping can be an almost-daily activity that requires walking and carrying bags or backpacks. Natural activities such as these don't put stress on your system, but they do burn calories.

When anchored, you can exercise while doing many activities. Swimming, snorkeling, and diving exercise major muscle groups and provide cardiovascular conditioning. Scrubbing the bottom of your boat may be something you've never done, but it is both excellent exercise and a productive task.

We don't carry bicycles on board, but many cruisers do; bikes provide transportation and good exercise. I've seen cruisers with inline skates, but there is a limit to their usefulness on dirt roads. Sailboards and kayaks are popular among cruisers with the space to carry them, and we have seen cruisers who bring tennis rackets and golf clubs. We have joined cruisers on the beach for Frisbee, volleyball, cricket, and bowling.

There is a temptation when cruising to socialize sitting down, with your elbow bent. Foods and beverages, mixed with the camaraderie of your neighbors, are tempting. But the result can be clothes that soon fit more snugly.

If you maintain a reasonable calorie and fat intake and make an effort to take advantage of the activities that cruising offers, you should stay fit. If you insist on being sedentary aboard and ashore and neglect to manage your calorie and fat intake, you may have a problem.

8

Children On Board

I HAVE COME TO BELIEVE that children who grow up cruising are the best children in the world in terms of their behavior, education, and appreciation of the environment. If I could do it over, I would raise my children aboard while cruising. But not having been a cruiser when my children were young, I can only report what cruising parents have told me.

We know cruisers who start families during their cruise and raise their newborns aboard. We have seen toddlers and school-age children who love cruising. We have watched adolescents blossom in the heady atmosphere of cruising.

There are parents who feel a boat is no place for their children, and there are parents who believe there is no other place for their children. If you choose to cruise as a family, you and your children must be happy with the decision and enjoy the endeavor together.

Nancy Payson believes cruising gave her children something that land life did not. "Two of my children were having problems," she says. "One had a run-in with the law, and the other was on drugs. They came and asked if they could go on the trip with us. They grew and matured. I really thank living on the boat for giving them the knowledge of their own self-worth. . . . They knew when they were on watch they were responsible for the rest of our lives. . . . They all learned things they never would have learned [on land]. They grew up with self assurance and a strong sense of responsibility."

Nancy Jewhurst and Nancy Bischoff offer advice and information about their child-rearing experiences. Nancy Jewhurst took her son, Kyle, then four years old, on a six-month test cruise to learn if she, her husband, and her son wanted to make cruising their lifestyle. The voyage was successful, and they returned permanently to cruising when Kyle turned nine. Nancy Bischoff spent ten years raising her two sons aboard.

Whether you live on land or on a boat, raising children is not a simple matter. Wherever a child is raised, that child still has needs and problems at every stage of life that parents need to confront.

Infants and Toddlers

Some couples don't want to postpone starting a family or going cruising, so they combine the two pursuits. Still, babies in the cruising world are few and far between. But we have the pleasure of knowing several couples who have conceived and delivered their children while cruising.

A Canadian couple we met chose to have their baby in Mexico. They selected a hospital and doctor in the Guaymas area, which is near the port of San Carlos. Just before the baby was due, the about-to-be grandparents flew to Mexico to be there for the event, and the entire family was present for the arrival of a baby girl. The proud father was impressed with the quality of health care and the modest cost. Doctor, hospitalization, and housing for the visiting families was less than $500.

Another couple had their baby in Malta. One consideration for expectant mothers is good communication with caregivers. In Malta, the entire staff spoke English. This couple also found that the quality of health care was far better and less costly than anticipated.

Caring for an infant, especially your first, can be very stressful. Not everyone is predisposed to deal with a tiny infant twenty-four hours a day. Depression, fatigue, and insomnia are common reactions. If you plan to have children while cruising, be sure you have some alternatives in case you encounter physical or emotional problems when caring for your newborn. A shoreside residence or someone to help you with onboard care are two ways to make the experience easier.

If you have young children who will be going along on a family cruise, think about ways to ease the adjustment for all of you. Take test sails together. Start with daysails and gradually make trips longer and longer. Use these trips as a way to realistically assess whether sailing with small children is for you and to learn what you need to do to make it work better.

Children love routine. When you move on board, try to continue some of the same rituals and schedules that you established on land. Maintain the same bedtime rituals, for example. Bring bedding from home and make room for that favorite teddy bear.

Preparing Your Boat

Cruisers planning to start families while cruising need to make sure they have adequate space on board and all the necessary paraphernalia.

A secure place for the baby while underway is essential. Newborn carriers that fit into cars have worked on some boats as a secure spot to place a baby. We have seen infant car seats suspended from the overhead that rock gently to soothe a cranky baby. Depending on the layout of your boat, you may be able to convert a pilot berth with lee cloths and netting.

As babies learn to crawl and walk, you discover hazards that you have never seen before. You will need to adequately childproof your boat. Go through your boat the same way you would go through a house. Get down to your child's level and look for dangerous areas. Your aim is to both protect your child from your boat and protect your boat from your child. Pad sharp edges that could injure a child. You can also round off some edges with sandpaper. Put safety covers on shore-power electrical outlets, keep tools and sharp instruments out of reach, and stow poisons and medicines in locked compartments. Make sure cupboard latches can't be opened by children.

Know which controls on board are in your child's reach. Can she reach stove knobs, seacocks, or the engine ignition key?

Remember that bodies and objects can move on a pitching boat. Are there any exposed engine parts that your child could fall against while the engine is still hot? Are there any objects that could fly free and injure her?

Netting strung through the lifelines to prevent little ones from slipping overboard is a must. Netting is not, however, a substitute for parental supervision.

It is important that your child learns to hold on as she moves through the boat. A young couple told us that the first words their one-year-old comprehended were "Hang on!" Make sure there are enough handholds.

Safety Issues

Safety training should be part of every cruising child's upbringing. Provide each child with a life jacket that fits properly. Is there a through-the-leg strap to keep the jacket from slipping over the head?

Is there a handle you can grab to ensure speedy retrieval if your child falls? Is there a flotation collar for head support?

Whether you are riding in your dinghy, loading at the dock, or standing on deck, every child should wear a life jacket; it should be taken off only when your child goes below deck.

When your child becomes mobile, she should wear a safety harness similar to yours. Most harnesses are capable of some size adjustment, but you can have extra-small ones made by your sail- or canvas-maker.

Think carefully about the safety rules you plan to establish on board. Be consistent and enforce them—both with your own children and visiting children. Make sure all adults on board know the rules and understand that they are to be enforced at all times.

Health Concerns

Keeping an infant or toddler clean is difficult in the best circumstances. Keeping a child's busy hands out of her mouth is always a concern, especially when you are traveling in places with muddy streets, minimal sanitation, and diseases.

One cruising mother told me the meat cases in the market were her son's favorite. The glass was so cold, and he liked to rub his face along the cool glass that was just about eighteen inches off the ground!

Infants and toddlers are small enough to be bathed in a plastic tub or bucket. Cruising adults can manage with saltwater baths and freshwater rinses, but young skin is sensitive, and salt water may be too harsh. You may need a watermaker or additional water storage. Prepackaged baby wipes are great for cleanliness along the way, but their availability depends on your cruising venue.

Make sure your children receive all the necessary immunizations as soon as they are old enough. Clinics and hospitals in foreign countries offer the same types of immunizations that you would get at home. Be sure to select a clean health facility that uses current serums and sterilizes equipment properly. Keep a record of immunizations received, especially if you are on the move.

If you already have young children, discuss your cruising plans with your pediatrician before you leave. Find out the best way to handle standard infant shots, what medicines in what dosages to carry, and how to handle the sudden fevers little ones develop. If you expect to be in remote places, make sure the doctor has a clear picture of the limitations in available health care. Ask the doctor for recommendations of medical books geared to children's ailments.

Babies and young children exposed to the sun need sunblock, a hat, and clothing that covers them. It is tempting in warm climates to let babies and toddlers go without clothing. Even if your child is sitting under an awning, the sun reflecting off the water can still reach him and cause sunburn. Skin that is burned, particularly at an early age, is more susceptible to problems later and must be protected. As children grow older and become more active, it becomes harder to manage the discipline of skin protection.

Don't forget about sunglasses for your children. You can have good quality children's glasses made up in durable frames. A way to attach them to your child is important; neoprene holders work best.

Diapers

The space an infant occupies is minimal compared to the space required for his baby gear. The disposable diaper has become a convenient standard on land. But storing and disposing of these diapers while cruising presents some problems.

Most new mothers prefer the convenience of disposable diapers to washing cloth diapers. Cloth diapers are viewed as a backup, acceptable only if there is no other choice. Two people I spoke with chose cloth diapers because of cost. In sunny climates with good access to water, managing diaper laundry was not a problem for either of them.

However, discarding disposable diapers can be a problem. Most cruising mothers dispose of diapers with the rest of their garbage when they arrive in port. If the diaper is so messy they can't live with it until they reach land, they rinse the diaper overboard or in the head before putting it in the trash. Unfortunately, there are many ports where garbage is collected on land and simply dumped back into the sea. Faced with this alternative, I would opt for laundering diapers.

Our friends who had their baby in Malta cruised on a 24-foot boat. They did not have the luxury of space for disposables, so the new mother hand-washed cloth diapers and hung them to dry in the rigging. I'm not sure how satisfactory this arrangement was for her—but I know her baby was rapidly potty-trained.

Food

Food is not a problem for breastfeeding infants. But toddlers ready for solid food and regular milk may present more of a problem, especially if you are in remote areas or on a long passage.

Ultra–heat treated (UHT) milk is available in most of the world, even in remote locations (although it is not easily found in the United States). Typically packaged in liter boxes (smaller boxes are sometimes available), this milk has a shelf life of six months. Once open, it can be kept in the refrigerator for three to four days. If you don't have refrigeration, you can use the remainder of the open milk to cook or make yogurt.

Powdered milk and powdered formulas are easily stored, but you will need sufficient water for mixing. If you are leaving the country, check on the availability of formula mixes (both dry and canned).

Commercial baby food is readily available in most larger towns, even in the Third World. Remote fishing villages and islands with limited supply sources are not likely to have the pre-cooked and pureed foods. You may need to resort to old-fashioned ways, such as cooking food and mashing it to make baby food. Vitamins for kids can be found in pharmacies around the world.

Your water supply on board needs to be safe for the whole family. Potable water from shore and water from the watermaker can work fine. When you go ashore for outings, be sure to take water. Nursing mothers, babies, and toddlers need plenty of water to prevent dehydration.

Social Life

Socialization for preschool youngsters, whether at home or away cruising, is often adult oriented, and living on board in a small space with your infant can yield fantastic results.

Nancy Bischoff believes that living in close physical proximity as a family is one of the benefits of cruising. "When we house-sat for three or four days," she says, "I couldn't believe how separated our family was. There's so much space. We were out of touch. . . . Raising a family on a boat? It's a wonderful lifestyle. I wouldn't change it. It brings the family together."

The closeness that results from living in a small space will give you the chance to know your child more completely and share more of yourself. The most obvious result among cruising children is the verbal skills they typically command at an early age. Without a continual schedule of television, babysitters, and parents who are always away working, interaction between parents and children is continuous. You will equip your child with the ability to communicate well.

Still, I believe twenty-four hours a day with a baby or toddler has to be broken up while you are cruising—just the way it is on land. Babysitters are often available. We have been in fleets where an invitation to practice grandparenting for the afternoon was a real treat.

Carry on board a variety of activities and games that your children can grow into. Even for young children, simple games and reading are important for early education and socialization. Keep in mind that books in English are more expensive around the world than they are at home.

Don't forget to pack the ingredients for celebrations: birthday balloons and Christmas stockings. Parties are enjoyed by all, and they create an event to anticipate and a memory to savor.

School-Age Children

It is important to understand the day-to-day needs of school-age children. When Nancy Jewhurst took her four-year-old son Kyle on a six-month cruise, she left prepared. With assistance from the local library, she was able to fill the boat with books—enough so Kyle had one new book each week. She purchased the Calvert home-study kindergarten course. Out of the 160 lessons in the Calvert course, Nancy and her son completed 19 lessons. "We just didn't have time, and he certainly wasn't bored!" she says.

Education Underway

Even though cruising is often considered an education unto itself, it is important to keep up with formal education while you are cruising.

The home-study program mentioned most by cruisers is the Calvert School, which offers programs for kindergarten to the eighth grade. The school was founded in 1906 and is based in Baltimore. Its programs are accepted by most school systems. (Contact information appears in the Appendix, page 161.)

Irene Hampshire was satisfied with the home-study program offered by the public school system in Oceanside, California. Her son Shawn, now in fifth grade, has been in the program since kindergarten. "When we are away on trips, I turn in work samples and I fill out a report card. When we are [on land], we meet with the teacher every three months." Home schooling has become an option that many communities offer, often without tuition or other fees if you are a resident.

Both Irene and Nancy Jewhurst devote time each day to act as the teacher. Most cruisers who teach their children aboard set aside specific hours and days for school. Successful home schooling requires the discipline to maintain the routine.

We discovered that everyone observes the standard school holidays and vacation periods, just as they would in a regular school program. I suspect the parents are just as enthusiastic as their children about holidays.

There is a growing movement in home study coordinated by

public school systems. Your local school district office is an excellent place to begin your research.

Health and Safety for Kids on the Go

Health and safety for school-age children depend on teaching good safety practices early on. Establish rules and be consistent in enforcing them.

Safety is especially important, because children are in or near the water all the time. Irene Hampshire, who is raising two boys aboard, says, "Falling in the water is not my big concern. It's hitting their heads against the dock or boat and being hit by other boats when they are in the water." Life jackets and safety harnesses are standard, everyday gear for many children. Enforce the habit of using these safety aids.

Bumps, bruises, and lacerations are normal with school-age children whether they are on land or on water. You may have to expand your first aid kit's inventory of ice packs, adhesive strips, antiseptic, and disinfectant.

Without everyday exposure to lots of other children, the rate of picking up diseases and germs from other children lowers. Still, kids still do come in contact with each other and share their germs.

According to one cruising nurse, cruising kids regularly pick up head lice from each other. She finds that kids play together and share clothes, and the bugs sometimes get passed along. Rather than discourage interaction among the children, she passes out tubes of shampoo for controlling head lice.

Also, making sure hands and clothes are washed is standard for the welfare of the entire family.

Food for Growing Children

Most cruising parents find that a simple diet works for the entire family. They use fresh fruits and vegetables and introduce new or unusual items as they travel. "The kids were not picky about food," says Gail Amesbury. "We [bought] local food, ate with local people, and it opened up a different environment."

"Whatever we eat is what we serve to Kyle," says Nancy Jewhurst. "If he doesn't like it, then he waits till the next meal. There's usually something in a meal that he'll like. A lot of what we eat is fairly simple, especially underway. Things like Dinty Moore and macaroni and cheese."

With this age group as well, mothers report that the ultra–heat treated (UHT) milk is ideal. Powdered milk is a hard sell with most children, because it is lumpy, and in many places, local fresh milk sours quickly.

Soft drinks and sweet juices are generally available in most countries.

In recent years, juices have been packaged in liter boxes similar to the boxes used in the UHT milk packaging. This offers a distinct advantage: Like-sized containers are much easier to stow.

Cruisers who do not have refrigeration on board can encounter problems keeping fresh meat, fish, and cheese for any period of time. Unless you are embarking on a long offshore passage, the regular trips to the local markets you will have to make are entertaining and educational for children.

Fishing is fun for children on long passages — and the activity keeps fresh food on the table.

Quarters for the Kids

Space requirements for school-age children can change weekly. Nancy Jewhurst remembers how, at age four-and-a-half, her son Kyle and his toys, books, and most of his clothes fit into a quarter berth that was six feet long.

Kyle is now ten years old, and he has packed even more belongings into that same quarter berth. "He has a big plastic storage box at the foot of his bed, and he can't stretch his legs out. But he claims that he sleeps with his legs scrunched up anyway, so it's okay. He doesn't want to give up anything — and yet we're going to have to."

In addition to the box at the foot of his berth, Kyle has three net bins against the hull in his bunk. They stick out about eight inches. One bin is for his clothes, one is for his toys, and one is filled with books. "It's going to be a real struggle trying to get him to give up some of those things to make room for his feet," Nancy says. "He's just growing."

A bunk big enough for both sleeping and playing seems to be the most common solution for growing children. A quarter berth is often allocated to a single child: It is like a small cave where a child can set up housekeeping. We have friends living on a Bristol 35; their nine-year-old son has the quarter berth, and their eleven-year-old daughter has the forepeak. Mom and Dad have a double bunk in the main cabin.

Getting Along

Before they set off, many cruisers express concern about their children's socialization, which normally begins on land when children start school. Once underway, however, few cruisers seem to remain concerned about their children's socialization.

I think the pressure for socialization and to be accepted by a peer group diminishes greatly in the cruising community. A cruising child sees himself less as a separate entity and more as a responsible part of a family group. Individuality is encouraged, because children are respected, given meaningful tasks, and offered the opportunity to be equals.

Cruising children always enjoy meeting kids their own age. "The kids interact no matter what their ages, but in order for them to truly have a lot of fun, the age has got to be somewhere around their own age," observes Nancy Jewhurst.

Gail Amesbury believes the issue becomes more crucial in teenage years. "After thirteen, they desperately need to be with children their own age. We've personally found that with any children we met, when we got them together, the liveaboard children didn't know how to play team games or mix with more than two or three children. They didn't know how to take turns at doing things. I firmly believe they need to be in the environment to prepare them for coping with society."

There is no guarantee other boats in any given port will have children aboard. It seems that more young people are cruising today, but many of them don't have children. Contact with adults is the norm for cruising kids, and they quickly learn to carry on conversations — regardless of age differences. For Nancy Bischoff, a less traditional upbringing outside normal social structures is a plus for cruising children. "Getting [our children] out of the mainstream is the best gift we can give them," she says.

Gail Amesbury offers a comment about socializing that strikes home for many cruising parents. "Cruising is a social life, and there are so very few children. If you're invited for drinks, there are no children. And most people don't enjoy the children being there."

Whether you are cruising or living on land, there are people who do not like to have children around. Entertaining or being entertained by those people when you have children is difficult. But I find that most cruising children are adaptable. I have seen them sit quietly and read, write, or play games while their parents chat without interruption. Those kids are always welcome on my boat.

Adolescents

Most of the controversy about children aboard centers on teen-agers. Opinions range and are sometimes confusing. The key issues with liveaboard adolescents are their need for space and privacy on board and their education.

Health and Safety for Teens

Health and safety concerns are minimal with this age group. The issue of AIDS is discussed by cruising parents, just as it is discussed by parents in many places.

The likelihood of injury is always a concern. As Nancy Bischoff said, "They could be forty, and I'd still worry." Her sons are sixteen and twenty years old.

Food ceases to be a problem. Most kids have learned to eat a wide variety of foods by this age. The occasional need to binge on hamburgers, French fries, pizza, and ice cream seems to be universal among young adults.

A Place of Their Own

Families with teenagers on board do face space issues. "Privacy is hard with two boys on a 33-foot boat," says Irene Hampshire. She has managed over the years. But now the boys need their privacy as much as their parents do.

Nancy Bischoff finds the living space on her boat adequate. But a guitar, electronic keyboard, drum set, and amplifying system, which the family plays as a hobby, takes up any extra room. On her 37-foot boat, four adult-sized people share very cramped space in order to keep their pastime alive. The pleasure it gives to the family, and to the people who hear them perform, is their reward for the inconvenience.

Most cruising boats with teenagers aboard that we encounter are in the 40-foot-plus range. At that size, it usually is possible for everyone to have his or her own quarters and privacy. Houses become cramped too, but stretching a boat to accommodate a growing family may mean a major renovation of space or buying a bigger boat.

High School and Beyond

Schooling presents diverse dilemmas and solutions. The main concern seems to be the need to prepare children for college.

Gail Amesbury's three children attended boarding schools in England while she and her husband cruised. "It was a financial drain to keep them there," she says. "It took away resources quicker than we imagined. Not only school fees, but every six weeks they had a vacation, and they flew out to where we were. The airflights were such a tremendous expense all the time."

Gail's son Simon was going to college, so his situation would not have been different if Gail and her husband were land based. Gail recognizes that her son Jon-Paul, age fourteen, could have been educated on board. But at fourteen, I don't think we could have coped with the level of education," she says. "We could have educated Rebecca on the boat, but I feel there is an ideal age to be liveaboards and benefit by it between six and thirteen. Girls, especially, need the companionship of a close friend to talk to and to mix in groups."

Nancy Bischoff is using the high school program offered by Brigham Young University for her younger son. (For contact information, see the Appendix, page 161.) "His high school recommends and accepts this program. We talked to his counselor. He's taking courses, and my husband is tutoring him. He's doing geometry, American literature, and psychology. We spend two to three hours in the morning. He gets help with geometry, and he does [the other courses] on his own. We haven't done any tests yet. He wants to do his senior year back home. We're doing his junior year over two years, and he'll graduate a year later. We're hoping it becomes less important [to return home for school] so we can stay out longer."

Irene Hampshire's older son Erik finished the home-schooling program at the tenth grade level. There was no provision for the last two years, so Erik began taking courses at a junior college. In order to qualify for college at age sixteen, he took an equivalency test and passed with flying colors.

One discussion about educating children sticks in my mind. Several mothers were talking during a break at one of our cruising seminars, concerned about their children qualifying for college. But in the discussion, they made several assumptions: first, that their children would go to college; second, that formal education would have more value than cruising.

The issue of formal education versus life experience is one that will be debated forever. Your resolution of the issue depends on your value system.

9

Folks at Home

L EAVING HOME TO GO CRUISING can be a relief and a liberation. It can also be a guilt-ridden experience. Separating from family and friends is part of cruising. That separation can be difficult, or you can work to make it manageable.

It is most important to prepare family and close friends for your departure. Réanne Hemingway-Douglass stresses the importance of family coming to terms with your decision to cruise. "Your family has to be able to understand what you're doing," she says. "You must get their support. You can sit down with them and say, 'This is very important to us. This is what we are going to do.'"

Preparation

As a first-time cruiser, you may or may not have a clear picture of what you're getting into. You've read books, equipped your boat, taken classes, and tapped every resource to get an idea of what lies ahead. In the meantime, your family has watched scary movies, read hair-raising stories in newspapers, and watched search-and-rescue shows on television. Your parents, children, and close friends may be certain that every kind of disaster possible will befall you. Your adventure is as clear to them as a trip to the moon.

"My father kept sending us clippings about bad things that happened at sea, but my mother was very supportive," says Réanne Hemingway-Douglass. I believe Réanne communicated to her mother the significance of her plans, and she left with her mother's blessing. If both parents had sent disaster clippings, perhaps Réanne would not have made the trip.

It is important to offset the feelings of abandonment and fear that families often have when loved ones go cruising for extended periods. The fears they harbor are not going to vanish. The farther from home you go, the more reassurance they may need.

Educate family and friends about what you are doing and include them in your planning process. Just as you prepare yourself with information and proper gear, you also need to explain to loved ones the steps you are taking. Pretending that nothing bad can happen while you are cruising is a disservice to you and your loved ones. Helping families and friends understand how you plan to manage the risks of cruising will make them feel more secure about your leaving.

Displaying a practical attitude about your plans goes a long way. If you have been gradually making longer cruises and trying different venues to expand your knowledge and experience, each of those voyages can be reviewed with your family to impress upon them what you are learning. Take pictures and keep logs.

Bring your family on board your boat. Show them your life jackets and safety harnesses. Have them try on the gear you will use. Let them inspect your liferaft. Explain how your emergency position-indicating radiobeacon (EPIRB) works. Whenever possible, take your family for short sails.

Age, infirmity, and distance may prevent you from having your family visit the boat or go sailing with you, but they can participate and support your plans in other ways. There are many things you need to accomplish before going cruising, particularly if you will be gone for a few years. Enlist your family's assistance in your projects, and more hands will make your list shrink quickly.

Everything from fishing lures to pots and pans, books, flags, and cosmetics will be on your list of things to research and buy. Ask someone to research which lures are best for catching certain fish. It may be better to make flags than buy them; one family member can take on a flag-making project. Involving family in new ideas and projects strengthens their sense of participation. My family helped me find the one item I dearly needed: a hand-crank clothes wringer. I never would have found the hardware store in Ohio that sold them.

Family can help by researching your itinerary and compiling information about sightseeing, history, and languages. Knowing more about the places you will be visiting will help them share your cruise. They are doing you a service and, at the same time, preparing themselves for your absence.

Communicating After You Leave

During short-term absences, regular communication while you cruise is the best way to keep your family happy. Calling from local ports or your cellular phone is easy when you are cruising in the States. As you sail farther afield to foreign ports, telephones will not be as accessible. (In the next chapter, I cover other modes of communicating during your cruise.)

If it is important to your family to be in regular communication with you, try to work out a reasonable schedule to reassure them. But make it a schedule that does not become a burden on you. I would caution you against setting up specific times to call home. One of the joys of cruising is your freedom and independence. Having to make a phone call at a specific time puts you on a schedule. And if you miss that promised call or can't get to a telephone at the designated time, your family may become worried or upset.

Your Feelings

Friends and family are not the only ones who will find your leaving difficult. Saying goodbye and starting a whole new life takes adjustment on your part. When Gail Amesbury went cruising, she sold her home in England and left her children in boarding schools. Initially, the magnitude of leaving home did not sink in for her "because of the excitement of the trip, the new boat, and the hectic times. To do it all, we went full tilt. Three months later was the first time I really had a down time. I missed the children. I missed the house. I was homesick and ready to give [cruising] up."

It took Gail about four weeks to get over the sadness of leaving. "I persevered," she says, with a satisfied grin. When Gail looks back, she remembers that the depression over leaving happened the first chance she had to stop and be still. When you are busy preparing and moving on to new countries, cruising is ". . . new and exciting. Then it hits you — the enormous step you've taken," she says. "In port, talking to other cruising women always lifts my spirits, even when we share our woes."

For Barbara Marrett, a connection to friends and family is a source of strength and joy. "In the sea of impermanence, it's nice to have the connection to long-term friends and family," she says. "One of the best things that I did was surprise my family by flying back from Fiji. The whole family had not been together at the same time for ten years. They were so excited. It was wonderful to be around the family."

Family Issues and Events

Being the caregiver for an aging parent is a heavy burden. You may be blessed with several siblings who share this responsibility, or you may be your parents' only source of help. On the other hand, your parents may not require care or may not want you to plan your life around their well-being. Whatever our situation, most of us don't leave home without serious consideration of our family's needs.

I told my sister when we left on our current trip that I would stay in touch as often as possible. Our father was ninety-two years old, living alone, and extremely independent. He had, however, suffered a minor stroke, which his doctor said was a precursor of things to come.

Six months into our cruise, my dad was hospitalized. His future was in doubt, and his days of independence were clearly over. I needed to help take responsibility for the decisions to be made, and I flew home. My dad did not want to accept being limited, and my sister and I needed to work together to get his cooperation. We moved him to a nursing home, put his personal affairs in order, and tried to keep him happy. I returned to the boat a week later. My dad survived for two weeks before he slipped into unconsciousness and died quietly. I was fortunate to be able to go home and assist.

My father-in-law died of cancer while we were at sea. We did not make it home to his bedside during his final days. Fortunately, we had seen him when our entire family gathered for our youngest daughter's wedding. My husband and I sailed with his fullest blessings. "We didn't raise you to stay at home," he told us, and we took joy in his enthusiasm for our plans. Remembering our last times together as a family is poignant, not regretful. Our last memories of him are associated with a beautiful event and a happy time.

I have been fortunate to have been able to field family situations during my years of cruising. You need to be realistic about your family's future and discuss potential issues with family members before you set off. Having a contingency plan for the issues you and your family might face is essential for your peace of mind.

Becoming a Grandparent

Special events, such as the birth of a grandchild, may warrant special plans. One woman I know circumnavigated, yet she was also able to fly home several times for the births of grandchildren. "I flew home from Fiji for a baby, and then I flew home from Darwin," she says. "We flew home from Cyprus, and then again from London. We had two homes— the apartment and the boat. I think we were very fortunate."

This cruiser was indeed fortunate, in several respects. Trips halfway around the world may not be in your budget. If you expect to go home frequently, set money aside for this expense.

Leaving your boat in a foreign country at an unfamiliar marina is not always a positive experience. If you don't know an area or feel confident about how your property will be managed, leaving your boat in someone else's care can be unnerving. Researching your options, as well as getting references from other cruisers, will make it easier to leave your boat for a trip home.

Disasters at Home

Being separated from family when disaster occurs is a frightening experience. We were at sea when northern California sustained a major earthquake in 1989. When we arrived in port on the coast of Morocco, a fisherman pointed at our transom and shook his head. Our home port of San Francisco, written under our boat name, was familiar to him. When he told us about the earthquake and its magnitude, we were stunned: Our oldest daughter lived in the area.

Being halfway around the world, we could only watch television reports that filtered through and wait until the telephone office opened the next day. When the phone rang in our daughter's apartment at three o'clock in the morning, her first words to us were "I'm all right. Everything is okay." She knew a phone call in the middle of the night would be from us.

Our phone call to California got through via satellite transmission while the phone lines in California were down, so perhaps we were luckier than those closer to home. In retrospect, we would have been frightened by the news of this disaster whether we were at home or at sea. The possibility of disaster is part of life, regardless of where you are or what you are doing.

Emergency Contact

I don't have a plan for emergency contact, so I haven't had to deal with someone wanting to reach us in an emergency. It may sound like we don't care. The truth is, we made a conscious decision not to have an emergency contact plan.

My husband and I recognize that any number of terrible things could befall our family. But we would not be able to respond immediately unless we were in a major city with an international airport. For me, knowing about an emergency and not being able to physically respond is worse than learning after the fact.

Your attitude toward this situation may be entirely different, and you can create a plan for emergency contact via ham-radio networks and single-sideband radio (SSB), as well as through satellite communication systems using faxes, telephones, and e-mail. (These modes of communication are discussed in the next chapter.)

We try every chance we get to tell our family that we love them. If we lose one of them, or they lose one of us, we know that we have said the most important thing they need to hear.

They Don't Want Me to Go

We spent time with a couple preparing to leave on their first cruise. Their family and friends felt they were abandoning their responsibilities and doing something frivolous. It was unthinkable, this couple was told, that they were not working or shouldering their social obligations. After some consideration, the couple realized their family and friends were not truly worried about irresponsibility: They simply were jealous.

Outrageous as this may sound, the reality of doing something that many people only dream about provokes amazing responses. Fortunately, this couple's commitment to cruising kept them on track, but it was not easy. In their letters, they told us they felt harassed and alone rather than excited about their adventure. They finally agreed that the message to friends and relatives needed to be straightforward: Please don't make us defend our life, because we are not asking for your approval.

Some people might call this couple selfish. Yet you alone make the choice about how to live your life. Making life choices in order to please others means your life is not your own.

Controlling relationships are established over a long period of time, and they usually don't start just because you decide to go cruising. It is important to examine what kinds of relationships you have before you make important decisions about cruising.

I know a woman whose mother has been an intimate part of her daily life for more than forty years. She expects to be constantly informed about her daughter's life, and when she is left out, she becomes ill. The daughter shared her cruising plans with her mother during the construction of her boat. But as soon as she and her husband left the country, the daughter was summoned back by her mother.

She is still undecided whether she will return to the boat or stay at home with her mother. This is a sad situation for her husband, who admits that perhaps his wife doesn't really want to return to cruise with him. Maybe his mother-in-law is just an excuse.

Families can also play a different role. Nancy Bischoff, who is cruising with her husband and their sons, says that her family "worries about our safety. But they don't say it to us. Just to each other. The whole family is very supportive." Nancy explains that no one family member wants to worry her with their fears, so they each tell her: "They're worried about you. But I'm not."

None of us would be happy thinking our loved ones didn't care about us. But I believe the attitude in Nancy's family is the important one to remember: Her family cares enough to worry, but they care even more that she enjoys the dream of going cruising.

Guilt

The most grievous thing that happens to cruisers is guilt. In some situations, it's very subtle. But in the end, guilt has the power to push you to give up cruising and go home.

The feeling of guilt is common after reading mail from home or having a telephone conversation with a loved one. When someone you care about tells you how much they feel your absence, they put you in the position of justifying your being away. Friends and family don't mean to put this onus on you. They are expressing a sentiment they genuinely feel. But you are missing from a chain of contact that is well-established, and your absence leaves a void.

Analyzing my own feelings, I realized that I was absent by choice. It was more important to me to be where I was than to be with my family. I still missed them, so my solution was to encourage them to come visit us.

Whether your boat is big or small, bringing family to visit can be a wonderful experience. "My mother had never been to Europe, and my brother sent her. It was a great kick," says Patience Wales of her mother's visit during a circumnavigation. Even if you have a tight budget, with a little planning you can afford tickets for the occasional visitor. In some families, it isn't a matter of having the time or money for a trip — it's a matter of waiting for an invitation.

Every member of my immediate family has visited us in at least one foreign port. We can accommodate extra people on our boat. Even so, we have had visitors who stay part time on the boat and part time on shore. Older family members like the convenience of real plumbing and beds that don't rock.

Having friends and family visit is one of the best ways to establish your love of cruising with them and alleviate their fears. And when they communicate how they feel about your absence after they leave, they often say, "I had such a good time seeing you. When can we do it again?"

The bottom line with guilt is your own attitude about what you are doing. If you love cruising, it is easy to share the joy of your experiences and turn your absence into something positive. If you are unhappy cruising, then guilt can drive you home.

10

Staying in Touch

PLANNING HOW YOU WILL COMMUNICATE with the outside world once you are cruising is important. Folks at home may not be familiar with the mysteries of communicating with a boat in faraway waters, so you will need to educate them. And ordinary tasks such as sending and receiving mail, making phone calls, and paying the bills will take on an entirely new dimension.

Who Forwards the Mail and Pays the Bills?

When you go cruising for any period of time, in the States or in foreign waters, you have to pay your bills, get your mail, and possibly have someone look after your affairs.

Some cruisers ask family members to handle these responsibilities. This can work if your relationship won't be damaged should something go wrong. We have a friend whose daughter pays bills, collects rent, balances the checkbook, and forwards mail. The arrangement works without problems. Other cruisers whose family handles their affairs have found that bills aren't paid in a timely manner or mail gets lost. Trying to get to the bottom of these situations can cause problems within the family.

If you have a family member handle your affairs, write out specific instructions about forwarding mail, paying bills, filing taxes, depositing income, and reconciling bank accounts. Give them specific tasks and deadlines—make it clear exactly what you expect to be done and when. Give that family member power of attorney.

We pay someone to manage our affairs rather than ask a relative to assume the responsibility. This manager has handled our finances and taxes for several years, and it was easy to have her take on the added tasks of forwarding mail and paying bills. She has our power of attorney and consults with our financial adviser on investments. We ask family to do one-time tasks, such as mailing Christmas cards or ordering and sending spare parts. But we draw the line at expecting them to work for us.

We access money by writing checks at American Express offices for travelers' checks; in more modern countries we use an automatic teller card. We avoid carrying more than $200 cash, either in dollars or foreign currency. If we need to make a large or unexpected purchase, we try to cover it with a credit card or travelers' checks.

All expenditures ultimately go through our checking account, because we use the automated teller machine or buy travelers' checks. Our manager uses the same account to pay bills, so we notify her if we spend more than normal. She maintains a checking account balance of $5,000 and sends regular statements with our forwarded mail. We pay her approximately $50 per month ($50 is her hourly rate), plus reimbursement for phone and postage and a once-a-year fee of $200 for tax preparation.

I maintain cash flow records to monitor spending, and I adjust our budget. At the end of the year, I print out a report and send it to our manager for tax preparation. She is an Enrolled Agent (an Internal Revenue Service designation), and she has our complete trust.

One plus for us and our manager is that she is a sailor. She makes an annual trip to wherever we are to discuss plans, review records, and tie up loose ends. We always manage to include sailing, swimming, and snorkeling during her visit—even though she is visiting us on business. We look forward to her visit each year.

When we spend an extended period in one place, we open a small savings account or checking account for convenience. In the States, it is a simple matter to transfer funds and establish yourself with a new bank. In a foreign country, the process may take several days. But you can use international money orders or similar tools to open an account. In a foreign country a bank account may be required for such things as visa renewal.

We have friends who use services to do mail, family to do finances, and friends to do taxes. We are fortunate to have one person capable of doing everything we need. When hiring such a manager, find someone who understands cruising and the reality that you can be out of touch for weeks at a time. Look for someone who has the financial skills to protect you from tax penalties and mistakes in accounting.

Some cruising friends manage their finances without assistance. You can arrange automatic payment of bills with a bank or financial group that offers management accounts. You can designate limits on the size of disbursements and frequency of payments, receive a monthly statement of your activity, and access money with credit card advances or automated teller machines. Cruisers who use this method have simplified their lives to the extent that they do not have annual dues, insurance payments, or other ongoing financial considerations.

If you will be on a long-term cruise, check with other cruisers to learn how they manage their affairs, look for advertisements in sailing magazines, and talk to people you use for financial and business services.

Start early in creating a system, to give you time to set up guidelines with managers and/or family members. Be specific about what you need, where you will be going, and how much you expect to pay.

Mail

Barbara Colborn reminded me of something many cruisers are not always prepared for. "Getting mail was very difficult at first, because I was used to getting mail every day. Getting it once a month was a real wait, but then when we got it, it was like Christmas!" I agree, and I must add that having the time to read and write letters is a luxury that life ashore rarely afforded me.

When you leave home, organize a regular system for having mail forwarded to you—whether you work through relatives, a friend, or a mail-forwarding business.

There are many mail services that can handle mail forwarding for cruisers. You can find individual services through cruising magazines, newsletters, and cruising clubs. Mail forwarding services that don't specialize in cruising clients are often less expensive because they have a larger clientele. One woman was very enthusiastic about an arrangement she had made with her local Mail Boxes Etc. franchise to forward mail for $12 per month (postage costs were extra). Many services will take on additional tasks, such as dumping junk mail, separating out magazines for separate delivery, and even handling bills.

Postal service can be undependable in foreign countries. I therefore use courier services, such as Federal Express and DHL, for important communications. The services are expensive but are more reliable than national mail systems.

In some countries, such as Mexico, cruisers press upon other cruisers — or guests flying in and out — to receive and send mail. With the United States so close and so many travelers in this area, it is a quick, easy, and dependable way to handle mail.

A *Deliverable Address*

How mail will be sent to you from home is only one part of the system. Remember that on the receiving end, mail delivery for cruisers is problematic. Postal services can be unpredictable. You also need to know where you want the mail delivered. Deliverable addresses are often unavailable, so it is important to research and plan specific delivery locations.

Some people use general delivery, marina, or port captain offices. If your cruise is not overseas, organize an address list and circulate it well in advance with deadline dates for mailing. Make sure you keep a copy for yourself.

Most of the time we use an American Express office as our address. They publish a directory of their offices around the world, which we give to family and the person who forwards our mail. In my opinion, there are several advantages to this arrangement.

First, the mail is secure until you pick it up. American Express requires identification, and each piece of mail is listed in a logbook and kept secure. When you retrieve your mail, you sign for it. General delivery in foreign countries, on the other hand, typically is put in cubicles or in boxes in a location where anyone can rifle through it.

The mail system at the Nicholson Yacht Charter office on the island of Antigua is a good example of a popular mail drop for cruisers. Mail is sorted and piled high in alphabetical boxes. If you have plenty of time, it is great sport to look through the mailboxes. But when you are looking for your own mail, it is mind-boggling. Mail is sorted on some days by last names, some days by first name, and some days by boat name. Most envelopes are airmail blue tissue, white legal size, or manila business size.

If you have your mail dropped at such a location, there are ways to combat the chaos. Instruct everyone to use a one-word name (we use Jessie). For ultimate convenience, if you have the opportunity, rename your boat so it begins with the same letter as your last name. Finally, tell everyone to use shocking pink or fluorescent yellow envelopes when they write to you. You will have at least half a chance of finding your mail.

A second reason why the American Express system works for us is that, after thirty days, undelivered mail is returned to the sender. In general delivery and port captain offices, I have seen mail that was several years old still waiting to be picked up. If I know we won't reach a location where we expect to receive mail, I usually contact the American Express office manager, inform him we will be late, and ask to have the mail held. Last year, Christmas mail was sent to American Express by regular mail. It was lost during the Christmas rush and arrived after our departure. After thirty days, it was returned to the sender. Our Christmas mail finally arrived in April, hand-carried from the States.

A third advantage is that foreign American Express offices have English-speaking employees who make it easier to ask questions and get answers, both in person and over the phone. They also provide other invaluable services, such as referrals to English-speaking doctors and legal services.

There are some disadvantages: I sometimes have to travel to another town to collect mail, because there is no American Express office where we are docked. American Express does not accept packages, so if I am expecting a package, I have to find an alternative service. I have an American Express card as identification to access services, but I have encountered other travelers who use their travelers' checks as a means to collect mail.

Electronic mail is becoming increasingly popular within the cruising community. I discuss that technology later in this chapter (see Communication in the Future).

Communication with Radios

Many cruising boats have a VHF radio and a single-sideband (SSB) radio.

The VHF radio allows you to talk to other vessels and land stations that are in a line-of-sight range typically about thirty miles from your location. This radio will help you communicate with boats in the area and obtain information on local weather, local shipping traffic, etc. You can also use it to reach local marine operators in the States.

If you have a single-sideband (SSB) radio on board, you can place telephone calls through the high seas operator while at sea. This type of telephone communication is expensive and is dependent on the high seas engineers getting a clear signal so the operator can place a call.

Use of the SSB is included in a ship's station license, which also covers VHF radio, EPIRB, and radar. The license is issued by the Federal Communications Commission (FCC).

Amateur Radio Operators (Hams)

With the right licensing and equipment, you can also communicate with the outside world via a network of amateur radio operators (hams). Through amateur radio you can connect via two-way radios to the telephones of families and friends—even if they are not hams. Talking on the telephone via ham radio is referred to as a "patch." You can put your family in touch with a ham at home for regular contact or use the radio to develop a system for contact in emergencies.

Depending upon whether you purchase new or used equipment, the investment in a ham system can be from $1,000 to $2,500. If regular communication is important to you, this may be a good method.

The FCC regulates licensing for amateur radio operators. There are five levels of licensing: Novice, Technician, Technician Plus, General, Advanced, and Amateur Extra. Each level requires an increasing amount of radio knowledge, and some levels have specific achievement levels in Morse code. Restricted licensing without requiring testing in Morse code has recently become available; this license limits voice communication to certain frequency bands. Many cruisers opt for this license since it is very simple to obtain.

For general information on amateur radio operator licensing, contact the FCC in Pennsylvania. For information about ham operation, classes, and exams, contact the American Radio Relay League (ARRL) in Connecticut; the League is a volunteer organization of hams throughout the country. (See the Appendix, page 160). All instruction and testing are done by volunteers with the Amateur Extra rating. Note: Amateur radio may not be used to conduct business.

We choose not to use the radio for regular communication because we do not want to maintain radio schedules or monitor the radio while we cruise. We also have a minimal electrical system, while transmitting via radio requires substantial output.

We have made it clear to our friends and family that we will write, send audio tapes, and try to telephone home at the beginning and end of passages and on birthdays. The key word here is *try*—not promise.

Telephone Communication

In the United States, we accept a telephone in every home as a given, but this is not the case in many parts of the world. Telephones often are located in a central office, not in private homes. We have found communication by telephone frustrating, since telephones are not always available in remote locations and the hours of operation of some telephone offices do not coincide with convenient hours at home.

My sister-in-law at first was convinced we were avoiding telephoning her. She did not understand the difficulty in locating workable telephone equipment at reasonable hours in Belize. After we relayed accounts of many dinghy trips ashore, walks through the mud to the post office, long lines at the phone office, and the eventual triumph of getting a clear line, she appreciated how complicated making a single phone call could be.

In the last decade, changes in telephone technology have improved service all over the world. Direct telephone connections via satellite and international access codes make it possible to place international phone calls from nearly everywhere, including simple pay phones along dirt roads or from the cockpit of your boat.

Cellular phones are now in use around the world. They have made communication while cruising in the States easy. Unfortunately, the technology of cellular equipment in much of the world is different from that in the States. You may have to purchase new equipment when you cruise in some parts of the world, and you can incur some expensive charges.

Most of the long distance telephone companies in the United States allow you to have a telephone credit card—even if you don't have regular telephone service. This is a breakthrough for cruisers, who once needed established telephone service to get a phone card. Long distance telephone service is available with regular credit cards such as Visa and MasterCard, but the charges are outrageous. In Mexico, for example, a normal credit card charge for a phone call to the United States is $18 per minute. The rate with a phone company card or local phone card is approximately one-third that.

Message services via regular telephone companies and specialized communications companies make it possible to have a toll-free number where messages can be left for you. In turn, you can dial a toll-free number and access those messages. This is an excellent way to handle emergencies and keep in touch with family and business. The only drawback we have encountered is the limit on message time with some systems.

Collect calls are simple with direct dialing systems, but they can be costly. Purchasing a local phone card that you insert in a pay phone usually is cheaper. If you have a choice, use collect calls or credit card calls as your last resort.

Communication in the Future

Methods of communication are changing so quickly that we may find ourselves beaming home, *Star Trek* fashion, in the next century. E-mail is very popular, and methods for using it are developing rapidly. Check with your local marine electronics dealer for the latest information.

Some cruisers are already using e-mail connections via ham radio, and SSB systems for e-mail and fax are also available.

I take my laptop computer ashore to send and receive my e-mail. I find a local coffee shop or store that will let me plug into their phone line. I access the Internet using the CompuServe system. Most merchants are eager to help. They may not understand e-mail, but they do understand accommodating a customer. I pay the cost of a two- or three-minute call and send and receive mail in thirty seconds.

One friend has equipped his boat with an Inmarsat-C satellite communication system. This system allows him to send faxes and e-mail from the boat while at sea. He and his wife can maintain regular communication with their family and business contacts. They can afford the technology, and they value the constant contact. The most recent price quote I have gotten for installing the satellite communication equipment is $5,000 plus the cost of a computer. The connection services charge about $4.50 per minute for voice, and about $.08 a word for text.

This system isn't in my budget now, but the technology will be more available and less costly in the near future.

11

Career Planning
and
Employment

WHEN MY HUSBAND, Jim, and I had our first serious discussion about long-term cruising, it came to a grinding halt when I posed the question, "But what about my career?"

His offhand answer, "You can always start over," offended me at first. But after my anger subsided, I realized that I *could* start over. I had many contacts in the large shopping center corporation that I worked for, and I could maintain work contacts during our five-year absence.

I planted the seeds for my return to the work force before leaving. I informed cohorts that I would be looking for work when I came back, and I completed a professional certification in marketing and management before departure to ease my re-entry into the professional world.

If you weighed what I gave up as a career woman against what I gained as a cruiser, you might not be convinced that I made the right choice. I gave up a substantial salary and the status and satisfaction I gained from hard work and proven results. But for me, going cruising was the right decision. I gained the freedom to run my own life, and I proved to myself that I could live without the safety net of a corporate career.

Facing the prospect of giving up a career is difficult. Women who have spent long hours improving their salary status, accomplishing important results, and gaining respect from their peers need to consider the choices carefully.

Some cruisers give up their occupations when they leave. Some view cruising as a sabbatical from work. Some find ways to blend their careers with the cruising life. And for some, the experience of cruising helps them make a career switch to an on-the-water vocation.

The Option of Timing

A career may be important in your life plan, just as having a family may be important. Remember, you have control over when you cruise and when you pursue your career. One option is to cruise first and work later. "We're 'retired' now. We'll go to work when we're sixty-five," says Lin Pardey, who has turned her cruising into a career.

University of Alaska faculty member Lael Morgan cruised as a young woman. People kept asking her, "Why are you doing this now? Wait, in ten years it will be easier." As Lael points out, she and her husband may not have had much money then, but they weren't encumbered with a house and family either. Thirty years later, her attitude toward waiting has not changed. "So many people wait until they're too damn old," she says. "I saw so many people who retired with more boat than they could handle."

For Lael the decision was easy. "It was his dream, and I went along because I didn't have a dream of my own. I never conceived of being away or taking that kind of time off. I haven't kept a straight job since." Now Lael is land based and works full time. Since cruising, she has written numerous books and won awards in journalism and photography. Ten years ago, she completed an advanced degree in communications.

Expectations

If you are planning to blend a career with cruising, think first about what purpose work will have in your cruising life.

Do you plan to work because you will need money along the way? How much money will you need to make? Do you want to work for your own personal enrichment or to stay current in your field? Is working in a cruising destination a way for you to stay in one place for a while and get to know the community? Are you looking for short-term work for extra cash or positions that will help you build your career?

If you want to mix working and cruising, advance planning will help you lay the groundwork. Think about what you want to do and how you will do it. Talk to other cruisers to find out how they mixed working and cruising.

Also consider the red tape. You should know what official statutes pertain to you as a foreign national seeking work.

Combining Work and Play

Some cruisers alternate working at their chosen career with cruising as a way of "having their cake and eating it too." They typically cruise to a destination and stay there to take on a work assignment. The key is knowing where you can get work and arranging the employment in advance.

In the South Pacific, a number of Americans find that American Samoa offers possibilities because there are no employment restrictions for American citizens. American Samoa's location allows you to sail for a couple years, stay in the islands to work, and then continue sailing at the completion of a work contract. The U.S. government employs people there in several areas, including health care, construction, and teaching. Cruisers negotiate these contracts in advance.

We met a couple in Pago Pago (American Samoa) who had sailed there so the husband could supervise a construction project for two years. The wife quickly found a job in retail. Her background made it possible for her to move up into management almost immediately. After a two-year stint, they decided to move on and see new places.

Other good cruising destinations for U.S. citizens who want to work and play are Hawaii, Puerto Rico, the U.S. Virgin Islands, Guam, Wake Island, and Midway Island.

Working in foreign territories is more complicated, but you may be able to achieve results with some planning and forethought. Before setting out, check library reference sections for employment information. Look for directories that describe job opportunities in different areas of the world. Information is also indexed by profession, and you may find areas where your skills are needed.

Teaching English is a popular job that allows you to work in a variety of countries. Requirements vary from being a credentialed teacher to being a native English speaker willing to fit into a school system. Such opportunities can be satisfying and typically pay well.

I have great admiration for a nurse I met in the South Pacific who was using her expertise to her advantage as a cruiser. Her training, including an advanced degree in public health, was in great demand. When we met, she had a contract that would begin in eighteen months' time in Saudi Arabia, and she and her partner were working their way to the Red Sea. Working in a strictly controlled Muslim society that limits personal freedom is unappealing to me, but her outlook was pragmatic: "I can be a nurse anywhere, particularly if they pay me $90,000 a year."

If a career is important to you, there are ways to combine your interests with cruising. Lura Francis had an established career as a painter, but it was very important to her to cruise with her husband. She sketched everything she saw while cruising and filled books with images that she planned to use one day in her painting. When she and her husband returned to California, they moved ashore. Lura used the sketches to recreate her cruising experiences in her paintings, and her one-woman shows were very successful. Now widowed, she continues to paint. She has expanded her career to include teaching painting and directing local art festivals.

In Phuket, Thailand, we met an American woman who entertained every night in a large hotel. She played the piano and occasionally sang. Having music in common, we spent time together in the afternoons talking about her work. She was one of several Americans we have met who entertain in restaurants and hotels around the world. In addition to a salary, many of these entertainers receive meals and guest privileges from the establishment, as well as tips from patrons. The biggest problem she had was getting regular practice time when she wasn't employed, so she carried a battery-powered keyboard to keep up her skills.

Technological advancements in electronic communications are paving the way for other work opportunities. Many land-based people work at home and never go into an office. On-line connection for computers aboard a boat is not as accessible as it is on land, but the capability exists. Satellite communication systems are being developed in more compact units with smaller price tags.

If you have an established career that does not require you to be in a specific location, consider taking the career with you. It would be hard to run a day-to-day business requiring daily contact with clients while you are sailing, but you could consider being in port during certain time periods to handle large projects. Or you might arrange work that you could accomplish on your own time while you are cruising and then deliver to clients as you complete it.

When is Recess?

There is a downside to cruising and taking a career with you: When your mate is snorkeling, sightseeing, and visiting with other cruisers, you may have to keep working.

I take my career as a writer with me as we cruise. More and more,

I am asked about writing as a career and a source of income. It is fair to assume there is potential in writing about cruising. The sailing magazines are full of cruising articles, and the shelves at the local marine bookstore are filled with cruising books. Unfortunately, the market for articles and books is small. What if you wanted to write about topics other than cruising? Take travel, for example. There are many magazines and guidebooks. There are also thousands of travel writers who are already established in the profession.

If you are already established as a writer before you set out cruising, it is easier to get published. As a contributing editor for a cruising magazine, Barbara Marrett uses her cruising experiences in her writing. "The key is to find what excites you about the trip, to have something that you can focus your energy on if just sailing isn't enough for you. I really like writing articles and taking pictures."

Becoming established as a writer is extremely hard unless you have regular access to a phone, fax, and mail service—and don't mind rejection. You need to find your niche, establish regular contacts with editors, and stay in constant touch. Even established writers must continually communicate with editors to get assignments and keep the flow of work going. A computer with electronic connection to the Internet means that research is faster, but articles and books don't write themselves. I love to write, but I know I have to skip recess—the snorkeling, sightseeing, napping, or partying—when there's a deadline to meet. And as a writer, I have learned that after every deadline, there is always another one.

Migael Scherer is a writer, and she points out what the difficulties are for her. "As a writer, I need time by myself. I can take notes, keep a journal, and write letters, but revising, perfecting, and shaping takes solitude and time. I can't write while I'm running a boat and cruising. The boat is a whole entity that needs care. I respond to the boat, the wind and currents, and what the engine is saying to me. I need to be aware of the boat."

Sabbatical Cruising

Another possibility that allows you to cruise and maintain a career is making short excursions on a sabbatical basis. Teaching is a profession that offers sabbatical leaves after a specific period of employment. Others find ways to make a sabbatical cruise part of their business life.

We know of a couple who left California to cruise for six months. They spent the time sailing and taping video footage. When the six months ended, they left their boat in a boatyard, returned to California, and produced and marketed the video. Six months later, they returned to pick up their boat and move on. This may be an intense approach, but this couple combines their creative skills and cruising in a way that is satisfying and profitable for them.

A young Swiss doctor who sailed with us filled hospital contracts that lasted six months to a year and cruised between assignments. She worked in the hospital when others took extended leave. She found the work interesting, and it was helping her decide what area of medicine she would eventually specialize in. This kind of sabbatical leave is not very common in the United States, but it is popular in Europe and Australia.

Adapting a career to cruising, or tailoring cruising to fit your career, is possible. It requires thought and creativity on your part, as well as the cooperation of your cruising partner. Not all professions can be easily adapted to life on a boat. But if you want to cruise, you may find some interesting solutions.

Making a New Career

When we came back from our first long cruise, I discovered that I truly could start over again and return to my prior career in the shopping center business. The problem was, I didn't want to. After nearly seven years of being barefoot and carefree, the appeal of a job I once loved had waned dramatically. The idea of dressing up every day, driving on the freeway, and spending the entire day in an air-conditioned office with no view and no fresh air couldn't compete with the life I had lived.

With a glimmer of encouragement from my husband, I began a new career. I combined skills from my earlier career with new information and experiences. I started writing, training, and lecturing about different aspects of sailing.

My husband suggested I try my new career for a year to see what direction it took. Working on my own terms and setting my own goals became a whole new way of life. At the end of the first year, I had gained confidence and earned some money—despite lots of rejection letters. My husband said, "Keep going!" The financial rewards were not as great as they were in my former career. But I no longer needed to drive a car or maintain a big wardrobe. The tradeoff was worth it to me.

On-the-Water Professionals

Some women are fortunate enough to have an on-the-water occupation.

Patricia Miller earned her 100-ton captain's license, and she and her husband John Rains work together delivering yachts.

Irene Hampshire and her partner live aboard their own boat, but they are responsible for a racing yacht kept in the same marina. They sail as crew when the boat is racing to a far-off destination such as Mexico or Hawaii. After the race, the two of them—along with their sons—spend months bringing the boat home through interesting cruising venues.

Dawn Riley is a full-time professional sailor and is in demand worldwide as a racing skipper. When she started out, she described working as a professional sailor as being "between jobs." The races and the boat deliveries became her job, and she eventually was invited to crew in major events as a paid professional. Not everyone aspires to this level of skill. But being an internationally known racer offers a career on the water and travel around the world that is extremely satisfying.

I met three women working with their husbands as full-time, professional charter crew. After years of cruising, they needed to earn money so they could continue sailing—and staying on the water was a priority. All three couples are full-time crew aboard privately owned yachts. One couple is on a large sailboat on the West Coast, and the others are on powerboats that cruise the Caribbean, Mexico, and the Intracoastal Waterway. My first impression of their life was that it was glamorous. But that is not how they describe their work.

When the owner is on board, work begins at 5:00 A.M. There is fresh food to prepare, systems to check, and watermakers to turn on. Their workday ends at midnight, after the owner retires. The crew then does the cleaning and the laundry. In some cases, they need to get underway because they must be in another location by sunrise. During their workday, they are deckhands, engineers, tender drivers, babysitters, cooks, dish washers, stewards, navigators, bartenders, and medics. This pace usually is maintained for a period of weeks, until the owner goes home. The crew can then be on their own for months until the owner's next visit. But in the intervening time, they must handle maintenance and repairs and perhaps move the boat to a new destination.

Working those long hours sounds like slave labor until you understand that the compensation for those intense ninety days a year for two people starts at an annual salary of around $65,000. Depending on the boat, salaries can be double that amount, and the crew's expenses are paid. In a few years, it is possible to establish a cruising fund of substantial size. This kind of career is not for everyone, but some cruisers have found that the financial rewards have afforded them a permanent cruising life.

Many cruisers carry diving equipment. They enjoy their hobby as they go, and they may find the opportunity to do salvage work, boat-bottom maintenance, underwater photography, and diving instruction (the latter requires certification, but instruction is in demand in popular cruising areas).

Peddling Your Skills

Learning basic skills—such as haircutting or sewing for sail repair—can help you create an interesting, portable career.

Your skills may be in demand in places where cruisers congregate because such services are not always available. Your skills give you the chance to meet lots of people and establish a flexible business that goes with you. The equipment and space requirements are minimal, making this an attractive option for some women.

Many cruisers carry sewing machines to do sail repairs, canvas work, and make clothes. If you are not experienced with a sewing machine, doing it yourself can be frustrating. For those with experience, the sewing machine offers a variety of opportunities for work. Expecting to turn your boat into a floating sail loft may not be practical, but the ability to repair sails in your forepeak or in the cockpit is very valuable. You will need to carry repair materials with you and keep your machine in good working order, which is not always easy to do. Working canvas requires a similar effort.

If you are a good seamstress or tailor, you can find opportunities to be creative, even if you are only making pieces for yourself or your own boat. The batiks of Asia, the hand-painted fabrics of the South Pacific, and the lovely textiles of Central America all make exquisite garments and accessories. Creating a unique product requires talent, but the items can create their own demand.

Beautiful clothing, artwork, and handcrafts produced by talented people who want to express their creativity are found in anchorages around the world. We met a woman in the South Pacific who had been collecting shells for a number of years. But her boat was small and her collection was growing rapidly. Her solution was to keep the most perfect example of each type of shell and attach a small, gold jump ring. She sold or gave away that perfect shell whenever an unadorned gold chain came into view. With each piece, she provided encyclopedic knowledge about the shell and its habitat.

Constraints and Regulations

There can be problems connected with careers and cruising. Just as the government in the United States has rules about non-citizens working, other countries have similar regulations.

Working in a U.S. territory or a possession of the United States typically is unrestricted. However, you can run into local biases. If you have skills that are in demand, a job is not too hard to find in these places. Indeed, some places are anxious to have skilled workers, even for short periods of time.

In foreign ports, working can be more problematic. Working without permission and being paid "under the table" is not uncommon in Europe, Australia, and Asia. Jobs waiting tables, tending bar, and doing repair work are readily available. These jobs may be short-term posts, but they are perfect for cruisers willing to take the risk and looking for quick money, not careers.

There often is work in favorite wintering spots, but those jobs, too, can be risky. Once, we were hauled out in Cyprus and working on our boat. Our neighbor in the boatyard was doing the same, but he was also doing small repairs for other cruisers. We were regularly visited by the local immigration and customs officials, who wanted to make sure we were not doing work for other people. Our neighbor was eventually caught and was expelled from the country.

If you want to find a job in a certain port, ask other cruisers what their experiences have been with local officials and local workers. Ascertain whether you are breaking laws or threatening local employment before taking a job. Most cruisers are given a tourist visa upon entering a foreign country. If you intend to work, make your intentions known. Failing to have the proper visa when you take a job can carry the same consequences as it does in the United States: You can be sent home.

Some cruisers don't want to work. As Nancy Payson says of her decision to go cruising, "I was presented the opportunity of quitting my job, and going sailing. That lasted for two years, until we ran out of money!"

12

Home Is Where the Heart Is

G OING CRUISING DOESN'T MEAN giving up a home. It means changing where your home is.

Each of us needs a home of some kind. The definition of "home" differs from person to person, but the old adage rings true: Home is where the heart is. As a cruiser, even if you keep a house on land, your boat is your home.

Your Boat Is Your Home

You and your sailing partner need to agree on the concept of your boat as home, and you need to give it the same consideration as you would give a shoreside home. A boat is not just your means of transportation from port to port. You sleep, eat, and entertain on your boat—just as you do in a home on land.

I am a firm believer in making my boat as homelike as I can. Take time selecting your boat. Take into consideration all the things you will expect from this new home.

Regardless of how big your boat is, it will never seem as if there is enough space. That is the nature of boats. You will be forced to make choices about what to have on board. The things that are most important to you may be books, a favorite chair, or a special set of dishes. If they are important, take them along.

There are, of course, limits to that line of thinking. It was clear my baby grand piano would not be included in my move to the boat, but an electric keyboard kept inside a special case fits into a safe niche on our boat. It is a first-class substitute.

Some women may liken life on a boat to life on the wagon train. It doesn't have to be that way. If you look at the boats of long-term cruisers, you may be surprised at the unique, personal atmosphere each cruiser has created. This is not accidental; it is a deliberate act done with pride and care.

Boat Units

You need to set aside enough money to create the kind of home that will make you happy. When I talk with would-be cruisers, I use a term called the "boat unit." I define a boat unit as $1,000. It represents the invest-ment to start the installation of each new system in your boat (please note, I said "start").

The expenditure of those dollars is usually focused on electronics, radio gear, dinghies, and outboard engines. But I encourage women to think in terms of designating boat units for the things that are impor-tant in making a home.

On *Nalu IV*, we cruise with crew or guests a great deal. The galley has to be efficient and easy to use. Refrigeration is important, because we eat fresh meat and poultry regularly. The propane stove has three burn-ers and an oven. There are salt- and freshwater foot pumps at the sink, and we have pressurized water with an electric water heater we can use when we are connected to shore power. We have stainless flatware and Corelle dishes for eight. We use placemats and cloth napkins and most of our serving dishes are souvenirs from cruising. When we discuss the rel-ative merits of purchasing electronics or galley equipment, my argument to my husband is straightforward: "Until you can show me a GPS or radar that will cook three meals a day, I want the best stove money can buy."

It should not be a question of a stove or a GPS. Plan your budget so you can afford both. Your partner doesn't want to do without creature comforts any more than you do. But the wonderful world of boat gear can over-shadow the simple amenities on board that we can easily take for granted.

Great Things Come in Small Packages

The practical considerations of planning your boat interior may not fit your idea of a perfect home.

Boats don't have movable furniture. The interior layout of a boat is structural, which limits your ability to change it. Just as a house has bearing walls that carry the structural loads of the roof and floors, a boat has structural bulkheads that give the boat its shape and strength.

Complete privacy on a boat is nearly impossible. You can have a boat with a separate cabin, but footsteps on deck and noises from the head and other staterooms are part of life. Areas of a boat interior can be separated with doors, but doors on hinges take up more space than sliding doors, canvas doors, or no doors at all. Complete privacy on a boat becomes a state of mind.

Moving Aboard

I think it is essential to live aboard before you set off cruising. It isn't always possible to move out of a house or an apartment six months, or even six weeks, before you depart. But if you do, it will make your adjustment to cruising and living on a boat much easier.

When you commute, you are still using your boat with a temporary frame of mind. Commuting to your boat on weekends allows you to bring extra things and take them home again. You need to live on board full time before you know what you can live with, in terms of the space on board, and what you will change.

Remember what it's like to move into a new house or apartment. If you unpack all your belongings immediately, put up the paper-towel rack, and put all your kitchen appliances in place, you often find yourself rearranging everything a week later. Getting the feel of a new space is crucial before making decisions about how you can best use it. And that takes time.

We moved on board several years before we went long-term cruising. In the first two months I filled, emptied, and refilled the drawers and lockers at least three times. My husband could never be sure where his sweatshirts and socks would be. Even now, just for a change of pace, I reorganize clothing lockers or galley stores if I think I can improve on the last sixteen years.

Selecting the Systems

Most cruisers find that less is better. Louise Burke, who has many years of experience at sea, believes that "The longer you spend at sea, the less you find you need or even want. Life becomes wonderfully simple."

The KISS Principle

There is a reason why some people keep their boats simple. The farther you venture from home, the more dependent you become on your own skills to repair and maintain everything on board. In our home port, there are mechanics, electricians, refrigeration repair services, and spare parts. In foreign ports, you may face long waits and huge expenses to repair even ordinary things.

Diagnosing the problems with onboard systems is essential. You can do it yourself or—if the system is complex—you may have to fly in a mechanic. The challenge of understanding mechanical, electrical, and plumbing systems is not for everyone. Weigh the importance of having refrigeration, a watermaker, or hot pressurized water against the time and skill it will require to keep those systems running.

What Are the Choices?

Some cruisers don't have engines on their boats; they generate electricity from the wind or the sun. Some don't have electric lights; they use kerosene lamps. Some don't have refrigeration; they use block ice when it's available. Some don't have holding tanks; they use a bucket.

The cruisers who live on those boats seem just as happy as the cruisers who have electric appliances, freezers, refrigeration, watermakers, and even washing machines. You and your partner choose how you want to live.

After many miles and many years, we added two luxuries to our boat: an engine-driven watermaker and an autopilot. These were not essential, but they were bargains we found hard to refuse. After we installed and played with the new toys, we got to know the peculiarities of the systems.

The watermaker can be run only in relatively clean water and must be used regularly. If we use it in dirty water, the filters clog. If we don't use it, it must be cleaned and "pickled" to prevent damage to the membrane.

The autopilot can be fine-tuned so it responds to changing conditions. But the more finely it's adjusted, the more electricity it uses. Occasionally, the autopilot's tiny brain malfunctions for no apparent reason, and it chooses to operate sporadically—or not at all.

Until we completely understand these systems, we will spend hours learning to operate and repair them properly. It is reassuring to know we can go back to our old, simpler ways without feeling a great loss.

I have made electrical and mechanical systems sound nearly impossible. But there are lots of boats with multiple useful gadgets and conveniences that are kept running. If you have electric power, then lights, a stereo, and video players become part of your life. With a watermaker, longer showers, pressurized water, and a washing machine are possible. There are appliances that run on your battery's direct current

(12-volt DC), such as blenders and vacuum cleaners. If you install an inverter that changes DC battery power to AC power (which is what you have in your house), you will be able to use drills, sewing machines, coffee grinders, and food processors.

You and your partner need to decide what conveniences to install and how many boat units you are willing to spend.

Comfort Comes in All Shapes

On the Whitbread Round-the-World Race, "A dry sleeping bag was luxury," says Whitbread skipper Dawn Riley. For racing sailors, a dry place to sleep and dry clothes are often the most important things. Most cruisers don't put themselves in those situations. They are living on board full time—not just camping out. In fact, most cruisers don't sleep in sleeping bags. "A boat becomes your home when you make sure it's clean and pleasant," says Barbara Marrett. "Replace worn cushions. Put down carpeting. Put up a few pictures. Sleep in sheets instead of a sleeping bag. Have real dishes instead of plastic or paper. And have it be your space."

What Barbara advises is possible on small and large boats. When she sailed on a 31-foot boat with John Neal, "there was a rug. The boat was very clean, and it felt like a home. It didn't smell bad. It was cozy and had beautiful wood."

Aesthetics are important, particularly to women who are cruising on small boats. Lin Pardey's *Taleisin* is less than 30 feet long. Still, she believes in having luxuries in her home. "I have a few special things from other countries: fine Victorian china, wine glasses, and velvet upholstery." Many women would consider those luxuries, whether aboard a boat or on land.

Some creature comforts are very practical, such as Nancy Jewhurst's desire for a comfortable chair. "I miss having a comfortable place to read, because on our boat we don't have one." On a recent visit aboard their 32-foot boat, I saw she had purchased a long plastic lounge chair to use on deck. It can be folded up and put away when it's not in use.

Many cruising women find doing laundry a problem. Paula Dinius invented a solution for taking care of laundry when they were not in a port with washing machines. "I got an ice chest and strapped it on the bow of the boat. I'd leave it for a few days. It would agitate the clothes [inside] and then I would change it and put in fresh water." Her only problem was washing heavy items such as towels and sheets.

"I found a little washing machine in Gibraltar and installed it in the shower," says Gail Amesbury. "It only worked in port, when we had water and electricity." Before she had the machine, "Laundry could be fun. We'd go to laundromat and meet people. . . . For the easy lifestyle, it is a small price [to pay]."

For Nancy Jewhurst, when you are cruising, "You have the time [to do laundry], so the things you don't have are not a major issue."

Lael Morgan cruised during the 1960s when creature comforts were few on boats. "I didn't miss anything, but I could have used a new library half-way across [on a passage]. Our boat was slow."

Nancy Payson enjoyed the improvements in her home as she and her husband changed from a wooden boat to a fiberglass one that required less maintenance and provided more amenities. "Initially, we did not have refrigeration or ice. And we had an alcohol stove, which by today's standards is primitive. As we gradually got things, I really appreciated them. Now we have refrigeration and a propane stove. You never have enough water. But I've lived with that so much you just appreciate being ashore when you can get it."

Giving up comforts doesn't seem to be a problem for many women. Patricia Miller said, "I just substituted 'boat friendly' material comforts for the ones I was familiar with on shore. I substituted functional galley gear instead of the mountains of marginally functional junk tossed into cupboards. I substituted sleeping pockets for sheets and blankets. Giving up the car and learning to get by with bicycles and public transportation was the hardest."

There is one other item that sometimes is missed. As Irene Hampshire, who lives on a 33-foot boat with her partner and two sons, said, "We could use a bigger boat, and a door to slam once in a while."

I Don't Need It

I expected the women I interviewed to want more creature comforts. Women who are planning to go cruising often identify things they believe they must have, but many full-time cruisers don't mention these items. These are some of the things that cruising women did not miss.

- *A double bunk that you can walk around.* A big double berth that you can walk around and make up easily at the dock is a monster in rough weather, because you can't wedge into a corner for a nap or a good read.

- A *galley with a microwave oven and a bread machine.* A galley with a microwave, bread machine, and pressurized hot water is still a challenge when it's tilted and everything is slipping and sliding.

- *Air conditioning and heating.* Accommodating the unit and its ducting can present a space problem. Cruisers typically want to preserve space for other uses. Most seem to feel they can acclimatize to local temperatures. In severe climates, such as Alaska, a diesel stove can be used for cooking, heating, and making hot water. Small, 12-volt circulating fans move the warmth through the boat.

- A *bathtub.* In warm climates, cruisers jump over the side, take a bath, and rinse off with freshwater from a sun shower. On cool days, a warm shower from solar-heated water takes the nip out of the air temperature. My favorite bathtub was a tiny freshwater stream in Malaysia. My husband and I built a dam, inflated empty boxed-wine bladders for pillows, and soaked in our private paradise until we looked like matching prunes.

Your Home Is Your Nest

You are the only one who can decide what will make your home acceptable for you. For some women, the galley is critical, since cooking is their passion. Other women want unique decor and colors that are pleasing to the eye and the spirit. Some women need plants and pets to satisfy their desire to nurture living things. Perhaps you need many different things to create a satisfying home.

Before we put anything on our boat we ask ourselves, Does it have two uses? This test does not apply to the life raft or the EPIRB, but it does apply to souvenirs and creature comforts.

My husband thought a hand-crank clothes wringer did not make sense. He argued it was heavy and hard to store, and I pointed out that it would make laundry easier, particularly with my advancing arthritis. He raised the two-use test, and I had to think quickly. I told him we could also use it for making pasta and rolling out pizza dough.

For Migael Scherer, "When you live in a small space, everything can be beautiful. Everyday things should be beautiful and everything should be nice. Frivolous things are good for the soul." She collects fabrics as souvenirs and makes cushions.

Cruisers' homes carry stuffed animals, sterling silver, native handcrafts, earring collections, and herb gardens. Those items can be useful, frivolous, or aesthetically pleasing. The spaces they occupy are big, small, old, new, wood, fiberglass, and steel. Different as these spaces are, they are home to each owner.

One of the women I interviewed grieved about the sale of her boat. She felt she had lost her home when they sold their boat and got a bigger boat for a different type of cruising. "I only had a few drawers in the aft cabin [of the new boat]. . . . It was a bigger boat, but I had less of me aboard. You don't sell something you love. It's like selling your soul."

Your boat is your refuge and your nest, and it can give you peace and security. Cruising is best when you do it in your own home.

13

Memories
and
Mementos

Y OUR BOAT IS YOUR HOME, but it doesn't have an attic, a garage, extra closets, or a tow-along storage locker. You are faced with hard decisions about what material possessions to keep and what things to discard when you move on board. Sorting and separating is never an easy task. But when you move on board, space reduction is drastic and managing your possessions becomes a tougher job.

Inventory Reduction

Our solution, although not planned, was a gradual reduction of items. Our first step was our move aboard the boat. This eliminated nearly all our furniture and carpets, major appliances, extra linens, and decorative items. With three children about to leave the nest, we decided there were some items they would want. We rented a storage locker and saved those items for them.

We changed to a larger storage locker twice before we even departed for our first long cruise. We found that household items were not the only things we had to store. We had every imaginable tool for building houses and boats, plus plumbing, wiring, and painting materials. Our boat had been used for offshore racing, and it came with an inventory of twenty sails that had to be stored. Over a period of three years, we managed to accumulate more things rather than reduce our possessions.

When D-day (departure day for our first long cruise) was upon us, we went through another inventory reduction. We turned over to the children the things we had saved for them. We gave extra tools to friends who could use them. We recut two racing sails for cruising, stored five spinnakers in a friend's attic, and sold or gave away the rest of the sails. We saved some materials that could be used as spares for the boat, and gave clothes to charity along with extra blankets, towels, and kitchen goods.

But we weren't finished.

We still had to deal with years of trophies, pictures, photo albums, yearbooks, and the like. A collection of souvenir clothing from a variety of regattas filled two large plastic bags. Sterling silver and pieces of jewelry loomed as a major problem. The hardest part had come. Some of the items we had to dispose of had dollar value, and some were valuable because they were linked to significant memories. Our solution was to keep most of these items, store them in boxes, and leave them with friends.

Seven years later, when we returned from our cruise, we retrieved most of our boxes and stored them in an office. When it came time to go cruising again, we gave away or dumped the items—we had accumulated so many memories in the intervening years that new memories displaced those attached to our old things.

Our oldest child has the silver. The trophies went to former crew members and yacht clubs. We gave away yearbooks and unused clothing. We sold three spinnakers. The pictures, both slides and prints, had increased twenty-fold; they were given to the children to sort, keep, or toss. We asked our oldest daughter to put together one album of family photos, including important events and places we had visited. We now carry that album on the boat.

We learned an interesting lesson. Memories and mementos keep accumulating with time. Unless we wanted to establish a collection akin to a presidential library, there was no place where all our possessions could be housed. And, it occurred to us, who besides ourselves would want the accumulation of our life?

I still collect wonderful souvenirs and mementos, but I have a different attitude about their permanence. The delightful lesson was discovering that I could manage those possessions and get even greater value out of them without keeping them forever.

I Might Need That

We all are inclined to think we need something and later discover that we were wrong. Your closet may be filled with clothes, but you wear only two or three items because they're your favorites. Still, if someone suggested you didn't need the rest of your clothes, chances are you might answer, "But I might need them."

When Gail Amesbury bought a home in Fort Lauderdale after the sale of her boat, she unpacked boxes of valuable things that had been stored in England for ten years. As she went through the boxes, Gail's reaction was, "I wonder why I saved all this stuff?" She has since changed her attitude: "I think you should cut the ties with the possessions you've got, because in ten years [they] won't mean the same [thing]."

There is a lesson in going through items that were put in storage years ago. At the time, those things seemed important. But as Patricia Miller says, "You don't know that you didn't need it until you do without it."

Keeping Valuables

The world of ocean cruising may not be the most practical place for some items, but that never stopped Nancy Payson from keeping a treasure. "I have my mother's sterling silver. I love it, and I want to live with it. Not that we're fancy: It's part of us." A choice to have silver on board may mean extra work. But for Nancy, it's more important to keep that memento with her.

You cannot cut yourself off from your past any more than you can disassociate yourself from your future. The trick is determining what parts of your past are important. "It's important to keep things that have meaning," says Barbara Marrett. "I kept little things that belonged to my family or friends."

What's Worth Keeping?

Measuring the value of things is difficult. As Americans, we are raised in an acquisitive society. I grew up knowing it was acceptable to go out and buy a gift or something for myself as a way to apologize, recover from a trauma, or perk myself up. Buying, keeping, and storing things is easy. That way, we never have to decide what things are really important and what things aren't. Reducing our possessions goes against the practice of accumulating. It requires us to measure the value of possessions in a way that may be completely unfamiliar to most of us.

Pick Something Small

"Your treasures tend to be smaller," says Migael Scherer, who has lived on her boat for over twenty years. "I have friends who have watercolors, pen-and-ink drawings, prints, and sculpture. I trade art with other live-aboards who have limited pieces." The size of those valuables has to be directly proportional to the size of your boat.

Some mementos are justified because they are functional. Our wooden pepper mill, wooden salad bowls, and fruit bowls are trophies we won. They are useful items, yet they kindle great memories and conversation.

Make a Choice

Think about how you would choose at a grand buffet table covered with everything you love to eat. If you fill your plate with servings of every dish, the result will likely be devastating to your digestive system. A more sensible approach would be to take a tiny serving of each dish or to sample a few favorite dishes. Consider applying this "buffet" approach to your mementos. Keep a tiny sample of each important item, or prioritize and select a few favorite items from the top of the list.

Saving Important Items

Even after the most discerning sorting process, cruisers often find themselves with things they can't bear to discard or sell. At the same time, they know there is no way they can take everything with them. At this point, they have to create a way to keep those precious items.

Homebase Storage

Long-term cruisers are reluctant to use the word "home" because their boat, wherever it is, is home. Cruisers therefore use the term "homebase," which can mean a variety of things. A homebase could be a storage locker in a home port, a plot of land in the mountains that will someday become a residence, or a small home left intact. We don't have a homebase, but at least half the long-term cruisers we know do.

Some cruisers are fortunate enough to maintain homes while cruising. Réanne Hemingway-Douglass finds a personal place essential to her well-being. "I like to have a homebase. If I didn't, I'd go nuts. I want to putter, to read, to have my own books. I like a piano. I love to cook." Another woman had to downsize substantially when she went cruising, but she still kept a homebase. "The thing I liked was being able to come home rather than moving in with the kids," she says. "I felt very fortunate to have this, a place to have our belongings."

For these women, the ideal situation was to keep a homebase where they could keep everything intact and return after cruising. Cruising women who do not find keeping a homebase an ideal solution have to search for other ways to handle possessions.

Borrowed Storage

Finding a place to keep things of value is not always simple. If you don't keep a base on land where items can be stored, you have to rent a storage locker or rely on family and friends for storage space.

Nancy Payson's situation is not unusual. "I couldn't bear to give up some things," she says, "so we stored them with my father, my aunt and uncle, and a friend. They each had children. My relatives divorced. My father forgets, and everything got scattered and divided up [among] friends. So much for things I couldn't bear to part with. They parted from me."

What happened to Nancy is common, because our mementos don't hold the same value for others as they do for us. A better solution is to ask friends or family to take the things that they really like. Migael Scherer used that approach: "I retained visiting rights to things we had to give up. An antique clock went to a friend. I still see that clock."

It may be a wise move to pass certain family heirlooms to the next generation when you leave. Barbara Colborn kept her heirlooms in the family: "David's daughter does have some family heirlooms . . . so we don't have to get rid of everything. Things are in good hands."

Safety Deposit Box Storage

There are some items you don't want to take on the boat when you go cruising, and they must be stored in a safe place. Items such as wills, copies of insurance policies, or expensive jewelry are best left ashore in a safety deposit box. Even though you're storing original documents, be sure to take copies with you for quick access. Migael Scherer houses her valuables on dry land: "We use the safety deposit box for valuable things. We leave photo negatives ashore and take the albums on the boat."

New Mementos

One of the great joys of cruising is collecting new mementos and memories. It sounds as if I am contradicting myself, but the truth is, you will find some wonderful items as you travel. If you have been selective in your original preparations, you will find the neces-sary nooks and crannies for new acquisitions.

As Barbara Colborn says, "When you go to a foreign country, there are just so many new things to experience: Why drag along everything from the past twenty years? You don't need it. You're experiencing new things."

Nancy Payson has a good attitude about new things. "I have accumulated such nice souvenirs from all the places we have been. The molas from Panama and carvings from the Marquesas and Tonga are associated with memories, and mean far more to me than the possessions we left behind."

You will find mementos and souvenirs that you want to collect but don't have space for. A gift of tapa cloth a new friend in Tonga gave me and a primitive handcraft in stone that Lin Pardey acquired would be fine on a cruise ship, but they aren't practical on cruising boats. Lin managed to keep her 118-pound stone sculpture by sending it to her homebase in New Zealand. The two pieces of tapa cloth (cloth made from tree bark) I was given were six feet wide and fifteen feet long and too big even to store on the boat. I gave one away as a gift, and I used the second piece as a wall covering in the forward cabin. Some friends thought it was sacrilegious to cut the tapa, but I would never have been able to enjoy it unless I found a way to use it. Glued on the bulkhead and protected with several coats of varnish, the tapa will be enjoyed for many years.

Another way to enjoy mementos is to use them to replace everyday items that wear out. Even if they aren't beautiful art, they may be unique because of the materials used, their design, or the memories attached to them. I use my mementos of Yugoslavia in my galley nearly every day. I bought a small, red enamelware teapot in a government store in Bar the night we arrived, and a heavy-duty stainless steel pan I purchased in Dubrovnik ended my search for a proper stove-top roasting pan. Blankets, rugs, and towels are practical mementos that also serve as unique decor on your boat.

Molas from the Kuna Indians of the San Blas Islands in Panama are colorful textiles. A reverse appliqué technique is beautifully executed in layers of colored cloth. Most cruisers buy more molas than they could ever use as gifts, pillow covers, or clothes. My small molas became potholders, which made fine gifts for other cruisers (of course, I kept a few for myself).

Cassette tapes of local music are souvenirs that take up little space and bring back great memories of places we have visited and people we have met.

Clothing is a great souvenir, as long as it is worn appropriately. In warm climates, it is tempting to buy clothes that are appropriate on the beach and in resort towns and forget that those clothes are not suitable in the local marketplace or church.

Shoes bought in the South Pacific are more practical for the area than the ones you might buy before leaving home. The plastic "Mary Janes" found there are very recognizable, useful, and indestructible. (It's also fun to walk up to a complete stranger, ask them how they liked the islands, and then tell them that you knew they went there because you recognized their shoes.)

My favorite new souvenir is a gold charm bracelet. It is so small it fits into an old-fashioned matchbox that I can store anywhere. Birthdays, Christmas holidays, ocean crossings, and other important events have been remembered with charms. A tiny heart my husband carved from teak when we were still at sea one Christmas and the tooth from a barracuda we caught in the Red Sea on my fiftieth birthday are two of the best charms.

Disposal Systems

You can easily accumulate more things than you can make space for. Lin Pardey describes how her husband Larry solved the quantity question when they first started cruising. "I love to watch handcrafts being made. Larry gave me a shoebox and told me to buy every souvenir I wanted until it was full. When it was full, I gave something away. When we left the boat and took a trip in the Kalahari Desert, I traded lace underwear for some handmade beads." Lin's box is bigger today, but she lives on a larger boat. She also uses the items in the box as unique gifts and thank you presents.

Shipping items to family and friends isn't always a simple task, but it is worth the effort if some of your souvenirs would make perfect gifts for folks at home. I can usually justify the purchase of an unusual item because I call it "early Christmas shopping." I enjoy the process of selecting and buying, and I gain great joy from passing on my treasures.

If you lived on land and tired of something, you might offer the item to a charity, a church group, or a local hospital. The same kinds of opportunities exist for your cruising possessions. I had a shell collection from Asia that outgrew the boat, and I found it a new home at an elementary school in rural California. I replaced a giant unabridged English dictionary with a smaller one, and the old dictionary became a welcome addition to the library of a Mexican high school.

Instead of using T-shirts or hats for trade, think about giving them away as a gesture of good will. Many places you visit as a cruiser are off the ordinary tourist track, and your visit will be well remembered by the items you leave when you depart.

The richest cruisers are the ones who have collected many, many memories. Precious things may be part of those memories, but things can disappear while the memories are yours forever.

14

Twenty-Four Hours a Day

A REN'T YOU BORED?" Non-cruisers ask me this question frequently. They ask because they cannot imagine what I do to occupy myself full time, twenty-four hours a day.

Barbara Colborn described her initial reaction to the pace of cruising. "I worked in an office. I wore heels, nylons, and nice clothes every day, and I had a schedule. I was scheduled from five-thirty in the morning until six at night—and suddenly everything changed."

A Different Pace

The change is not a lack of activity. There are different activities when you go cruising, running at a different pace according to a new set of priorities. The first thing I do at the start of a cruise is remove my wristwatch. On shore, we jam so many obligations into a day: keeping appointments; picking kids up after school; getting to the store before it closes. There is no hope of getting everything done without monitoring the progress of the day with a wristwatch.

On the boat, I want to control my time rather than have it control me. Cruising offers me the opportunity to set my own schedule and move at my own pace.

We still need to keep track of time on board. We have two clocks on the boat: one set to local time and one set to universal time, which is the same as Greenwich time (or coordinated universal time). The latter clock is useful for keeping track of international broadcasts, weatherfax schedules, or making sure our log keeping is consistent as we cross time zones. The local time clock is useful for knowing when tides and currents change and when the local market opens. The clocks are also important for our system of watch keeping.

I don't need a clock to tell me if it is time to eat or sleep: My body handles those tasks. Social invitations happen "around sunset, or when you see the dinghy back at the boat." If you are more comfortable wearing a watch on board, do so. But let your body and your environment also have a say in your schedule.

I had a friend who wore a watch without hands. The face moved, and a little notch in the face revealed a rainbow of colors underneath. She couldn't tell if she was five minutes early or five minutes late. She kept time based on whether something was blue, lavender, or pink. It was the perfect watch for cruising.

You may wear a watch because you want to keep a schedule. But when you are cruising, you will likely find people who don't value time in the same way you do.

At home, you expect to pick up your laundry on a specific day, at a specific time. Rarely does your laundry service fail you. If they do, they know you will take your business elsewhere. But in some countries, it is not really important if you have clean clothes today at two o'clock or tomorrow at ten o'clock. You will get your clean clothes, but you may not get them when you thought they were promised. And no matter what you say or do, you won't change deeply rooted local customs so that they conform to your schedule.

In some warm countries we have visited, activities cease during the hottest part of the day. I had to learn to live with the flow. We met a cruising couple in Mexico who worked as entertainers in a local restaurant. They worked from eleven o'clock at night until four o'clock in the morning. For some, the prospect of staying up all night to entertain—or to be entertained—is preposterous. Yet, if you sleep through the heat of the day, dining late and dancing all night do make some kind of sense.

Americans have a reputation for being impatient. We don't expect to wait for service, meals, appointments, or people. When we think things need to happen more quickly, our solution is to offer money to grease the wheels of progress. I have had officials tell me they can't accomplish a given task on time, which may mean they expect me to pay for faster service. When I tell them I don't mind waiting, I usually get whatever I need in a timely manner.

Part of cruising is being willing to change your pace and your attitude. Learning to eat when you want to eat or sleep when you want to sleep may be hard to do if a clock has always dictated your habits. But even if you are on a short cruise, try to put your watch away and leave your time open rather than packed with commitments. You may be pleased with the results.

Schedules for Sailing

I said that your time is your own when you cruise. But I have to backtrack. When you are underway, your boat and Mother Nature determine the sequence of events. You order your day with a variety of activities, yet you know that at any time, plans may change: The weather changes, sea conditions change, boat gear breaks down. There are schedules to keep as you sail, including your watch system and set hours for radio nets.

Standing Watch

Our watch system is ordinarily two hours on and two hours off at night. During the daylight hours, we switch to four hours on and four hours off. Sailing at night is very pleasant. But because it is hard work to pay attention at night, we do shorter watches. This way, over the course of the night, each of us gets a total of four hours sleep in two two-hour blocks of time. We also take naps during the day.

I love the early morning, and I prefer the watches from midnight to 2:00 A.M. and 4:00 to 6:00 A.M. My husband is a night owl, so he is on watch until midnight and then takes the 2:00 to 4:00 A.M. shift. Our pattern usually works well.

When I go off watch at six in the morning, I will not be on the helm again until 10 A.M. If I'm really tired, I sleep for an hour, get up to make breakfast, then read or write or go back to sleep. Or if I am very awake at 6 A.M., I make breakfast, then sit in the cockpit to chat. When my husband goes off watch at 10 A.M., he usually sleeps for an hour or two, washes the breakfast dishes, and makes lunch. When I go off watch at 2 P.M., I like to handle specific boat tasks. If we are busy doing sail changes, I stay on to help out. By late afternoon, I want to do two things: get cleaned up and organize our evening meal. When I go back on watch at 6 P.M., we have a glass of wine, and Jim gets cleaned up and serves dinner. He often reads or catches a quick nap and does the dishes before going on watch at 10 P.M.

At the 10 P.M. watch change we discuss things that are important for the upcoming night. We keep hot water in a thermos for chocolate or coffee, and there are cookies or candy for a sugar charge on watch. If it looks as if the wind will get stronger during the night, we might put a reef in the mainsail or change the jib. We don safety gear and discuss any navigation issues—particularly if we are sailing inland or close to a coastline.

We maintain the same pattern in heavy weather, except the person off watch sleeps on deck during the night. This allows either of us to respond quickly in case there is a problem. When there are only two people on board, safety harnesses are absolutely essential at night. In rough weather, harnesses are worn around the clock, in the cockpit and on deck.

I am always surprised when cruisers tell me they sit and read a book or watch videos in the cabin during their watch and come on deck to look around every once in awhile. Keeping a proper lookout requires being on deck. We don't use earphones on watch. They can block out the sound of the wind, buoys, or a running engine. In bad weather, with reduced visibility and the potential for problems, it is most crucial that someone be on deck continuously, watching and listening to the boat.

We keep a log during passages, recording wind velocity, wind direction, barometric pressure, course steered, boat speed, and time of day. It helps us monitor our progress. It also helps us track regular patterns in the weather. We always include comments in the log, so the person who was off watch knows what happened while he or she was asleep.

Stick to a schedule that distributes work and rest equitably, whether you are daysailing or making long trips. My husband has generous moments when he decides to stay on watch an extra hour to give me more sleep. But it doesn't work because my body clock knows when I have to be on watch. When it's your turn to sleep, rather than being a nice guy and letting the other person sleep, make the watch change on time. You need the rest, and the other person probably would not sleep soundly because his body clock says it's time to get up.

It generally takes three days to fully adjust to a watch system. If you have trouble sleeping during the day, try eye shades. Even if you don't sleep, use the time to rest and relax. Your body will respond, and you will adjust more easily to the schedule.

Off Watch

What the person who is off watch needs most is sleep. Making sure you get sufficient sleep is as important as being able to stay awake on watch.

Still, there is time to do more than sleep when you are off watch. As Barbara Colborn said when she returned from her first ocean cruise, "On our passages, especially with the four-hour watches, I'd have plenty of time by myself, and we would of course both be awake at certain times. We'd sit and talk and have wonderful times together."

On some boats, the off-watch person does the cooking. If only one person assumes responsibility for cooking, then a system needs to be developed so meals can be cooked without infringing on anyone's sleep.

The off-watch person can use waking time to take care of personal needs, monitor radio broadcasts, and handle minor repairs. He or she should take care of the cleanup when not cooking, so one person doesn't do all the domestic chores.

Off-watch hours on long passages offer great opportunities. I have taught crew how to knit on long passages. One morning one of our crew said he missed bagels terribly. We spent our off watch together making bagels. By the end of the passage he was the expert. I put the sewing machine on deck during a pre-Christmas passage and made Christmas stockings for everyone.

Nets

Amateur radio operators, referred to as hams, participate in nets. Communication at scheduled times on certain radio bands is organized by general geographic area. The hams congregate on the net to exchange information on weather, offer or ask for assistance with a problem, and gossip about which boats are sailing where. The first minute is always cleared for emergency transmissions. If you are in trouble, ham or not, you can get on the radio and ask for help.

Informal, short-term nets often are formed when several boats plan to make a passage at the same time. The boats agree to communicate at a pre-arranged time on VHF, single-sideband, or ham radios.

The exercise is particularly good if you are sailing through unfamiliar waters. Faster boats can advise slower boats of changing weather and can let others know if there are any problems with port clearances.

In recent years, I have found more and more boats participating in these informal nets, particularly on VHF radio.

Weatherfax

Receiving weather information via a weatherfax requires maintaining a schedule, although the weatherfax can be preprogrammed just as you preprogram your VCR to tape a favorite television show. Weatherfaxes provide satellite images and hand-drawn interpretations of images.

Normally, they present current conditions and rough projections for the next twelve, twenty-four, and forty-eight hours. This information can be especially useful during hurricane seasons or when planning a passage.

Time at Anchor

I have heard it estimated that most cruisers spend about thirty percent of their time underway and about seventy percent of their time in port. You can find boats that don't fit that ratio, but—even so—the estimate raises a key question: When you are not sailing, what do you do?

When cruising no longer is your vacation or a short-term experience and becomes your life, how you use the time at anchor becomes an important matter.

Everyday Life in Port

I asked Nancy Jewhurst, who is cruising on her 32-foot boat with her husband and son, to describe what she does on a typical day at anchor. "The same thing everyone does in their homes everywhere," she answered.

Like many people the world over, her day is focused on taking care of everyday needs. "I get up in the morning, cook breakfast, and spend half the day doing school[work] with Kyle. I do laundry, although there is less of it in a climate where you're not wearing too many clothes. Make lunch. Go shopping for food, which when you're cruising takes about four times as long as it does when you're living on land with a car."

As a cruiser, you don't just hop into your car and drive off to the store to pick up a few items. As Nancy explains, "You get into your dinghy, and row your dinghy to shore. You tie your dinghy up, making sure it's safe. You walk to the store—you might take a taxi—but you probably walk. You load up with groceries—if you have too many, you might take a taxi—and walk back. Load all that stuff in your dinghy, go back to your boat, unload it, and put it away. Now that's a long process."

Shopping can be an Olympic exercise. It can also be part of the fun and entertainment of cruising. We wanted fresh garden vegetables after an eighteen-day passage from Mexico to the Marquesas. A local said he would take us to a place where we could get everything we wanted. We hiked up a steep mountain road for forty-five minutes and finally arrived at a huge garden that was terraced on the mountainside. We picked our own lettuce, beans, onions, brussels sprouts, and spinach. It was much more than a shopping trip.

In many cruising venues, there are no supermarkets. Outdoor, farmer-style markets are common around the world. They are colorful, fun to use, but limited because they normally carry only fresh produce, meats, poultry, fish, and maybe bread. Staples in bags, bottles, and cans are more likely to be found in small stores. Coffee, tea, wine, beer, soda, and dairy products typically are in a third location. Cleaning materials and paper items might be purchased in yet another place.

I have spent an entire day doing the shopping in foreign countries. After making a list of what I needed, I had to translate the list into another language, study the currency, learn to count in the language, and learn how to ask questions. "How much?" and "Is it ripe?" are usually at the top of the list. Part of the enjoyment is knowing that the next trip ashore could be the story of the day. Stopping in the market to watch a local festival unfold or following a big turtle swimming across the cove can be part of that typical day in port.

Destinations

For many cruisers, reaching a destination is the reason for making a passage. A spectacular city, an ancient ruin, or a world-famous dive spot are the kinds of locales that draw people from around the world.

Most cruisers find there is not enough time to sample all a place has to offer and still handle necessary tasks such as boat maintenance, repairs, and housekeeping on board. I asked one woman if she was interested in joining a group of women who walked every morning for exercise. She looked stunned and responded, "I can't possibly squeeze in another thing. I just don't see how some women do it all." I neglected to tell her the destination was usually the market, so the exercise excursion was an outing that rolled fitness and chores into one.

The minute I discovered that a planned maintenance stop in Mexico would be prolonged due to lack of paint, I hired a tutor to help me improve my Spanish. Her hours were flexible, and she charged me $5.50 for a two-hour session each afternoon. Not only did my Spanish improve, but I learned about new markets, local festivals and events, menus to test, and my tutor's family. It was an unexpected opportunity from which I gained numerous benefits.

One comment about cruisers' activities from Patricia Miller is important to repeat here. "My first season cruising in Mexico, booze pervaded everyone's lifestyle, because we couldn't figure out why we weren't satisfied." She found that people had looked forward to cruising but they didn't know what to do with their non-sailing time except drink. There is always something to see or do, but you are your own motivator and inspiration. You can sit and do nothing—or you can fill your time with lots of activity. Look around to figure out what satisfies you.

Making Friends

At almost every anchorage, you will discover old friends and make new ones, and an important aspect of anchor time is socializing. "I didn't realize I would meet so many people and make so many friends from every walk of life," says Gail Amesbury. "It opens your eyes to the outside world."

We met Gail and her husband via radio contact during our Atlantic crossing. We traveled together for several months as nodding acquaintances, until they invited us to join them in bowling on the green— which turned out to be bowling on the beach. We spent several hours laughing and giggling together as we broke every rule of this "staid" English pastime. Although separated by many miles and years, we keep regular contact and share a special friendship.

Some cruisers exchange cards and collect them as mementos. We have a notebook that we ask other cruisers to write in. We ask for specific things—such as home addresses or comments on the locale and our shared experiences there. We paste a picture or their card on the page to help us remember them later.

Among cruisers, informal schedules develop around many activities. Afternoon snorkeling is best because the sun is just right or the air temperature is the hottest. Jogging, walking, or running is best early in the day or at sundown—because the weather is cooler. Fishing is good just after sunrise or just before sunset, since the fish can see the bait better.

Radio nets also serve a purpose when you are in port. In some popular cruising ports, everyone in an anchorage turns on the VHF at sunrise to ask questions, welcome newcomers, and share jokes. The nets are a good way to hook into the cruising community in port, giving new cruisers an immediate sense of belonging.

At home, an enclosed yard, patio, or life indoors minimizes your contact with people next door. Business contacts—yours or his—may be part of your social life, but the friendship usually is limited because it is the focus of one person. Stopping to assist strangers is considered a dangerous practice.

When you are cruising, you easily establish common bonds with other people. You share meals, drinks, bad weather, dragging anchors, and lost dinghies. Even though you may only know each others' first names, you can have more in common with those fellow cruisers than most people have with longtime neighbors or business associates.

Among cruisers, friendships are strong because the basic rule is this: Take care of each other and always offer assistance. The problem of one boat becomes the problem of the entire fleet. If you have skills, you offer them. When you need help, your fellow cruisers offer assistance.

We were in the Caribbean when a catamaran lost her power and needed help to get into Rodney Bay on St. Lucia. Teaming up with another cruiser, we both put dinghies in the water, positioned the dinghies on each side of the catamaran, and maneuvered the boat through the channel and into the boatyard slip. Just as we were finishing the job, the transom of our dinghy collapsed. The other dinghy and the catamaran skipper got us to the beach before we lost our dinghy and our outboard engine.

Friendships lead to socializing that is fun and worthwhile. We come away from every occasion having learned something new or having heard a different point of view on a long-held notion. These friendly gatherings occur on the street, in dinghies, in restaurants, in cockpits, or along the beach. Unscheduled and informal, they fill hours and days with amusement and information.

Friends from Home

When we first started cruising, friends from home wanted to join us at various destinations along the way. We enjoyed one rendezvous after the next with several sets of friends. But it soon became clear that we were not in control of our cruise as long as we had to meet the schedules of others. So we set new parameters for guests.

We would give friends an arrival date and location with the proviso that we would be within one hundred miles (about a day's travel) of the location when they arrived, depending on the weather. We would leave word at a designated place about when and where to meet us.

We required one more change in planning: Guests had to allow a minimum of three weeks of cruising time. We hated sailing away from a lovely cove or interesting village to meet plane departures. We discovered that, with this change, we were happier because our guests had to be flexible with us. This change weeded out visitors who needed to adhere to strict schedules. And those who came to cruise easily shifted gears to our pace, rather than expecting us to keep to their schedules.

Will I Be Bored?

Only one of the cruising women I interviewed said she was bored some of the time. The rest of the women proclaimed their love for the cruising lifestyle. If you have the need to fill every moment of the day with planned activities, you may find that cruising is not for you.

In order to find out what cruising can be like, you need to let go of your old life, your old ways, your old schedule, and—maybe—your old wristwatch.

"I think the way to live is the way you live when you're cruising, which is to do everything at a slower pace," says Nancy Jewhurst. "You look around as you're doing it. You smell things. The number of things you have to do when you're cruising is much smaller, so you can afford to take the time to go at them more slowly. . . . There's usually no need to rush."

15

Woman to Woman

B AD HAIR DAYS MAY BE A JOKE to some. But those days can make me feel miserable. Each of us has a particular trait that seems to be the stem from which confidence blossoms or fails. Hair is not of grave importance, but if the reflection in the mirror looks grim, it's hard not to have a rotten day.

Your focus in the mirror may be your clothes, your figure, or wrinkles in your skin. But, you may wonder, is appearance important while you are cruising?

That answer depends on the individual woman. To assume that all cruisers prefer to look shabby and unkempt is wrong. Yet cruisers are not constantly bathing, shampooing, and changing their clothes.

Deciding to stop wearing makeup, getting permanents, or bathing every day is your choice. But if your physical appearance directly affects your sense of self, then knowing how to take care of yourself at sea is important.

Bathing

Patience Wales has cruised many miles, and her attitude toward bathing remains unchanged. "You learn to bathe in salt water and learn to conserve. You even conserve when you have a watermaker. We had a big 42-foot ketch, and we didn't go very fast. What you do is take a bath every day. . . . I couldn't imagine not taking one. You feel clean. You take two cups of water and a face cloth and go up on the foredeck and you get clean. I have sailed with people who simply don't bathe, and I think it's awful. You feel so much better." Two cups of water may not sound like a bath. But on a long passage with a limited water supply, it's a luxury.

The idea that you can bathe in salt water is hard for some people to accept, but it is how many of us stay clean, especially in tropical latitudes. As Patricia Miller says, "I loved bathing in the ocean with special soaps before rinsing with fresh water in the cockpit."

"I enjoy bathing in the ocean. It was one of the things I missed: jump over the side and take a bath. A bathroom fogs up," says Paula Dinius (who made me wonder why I don't just stand under the garden hose, even on land).

Louise Burke points out another aspect of bathing that makes the whole prospect extremely romantic. "During passages . . . bathing and shampooing may be on deck with Prell and liquid Joy . . . topped off with a brisk toweling. It's refreshing, bohemian, and can be fun if you help each other in the waning twilight as your new home whisks you off to a new adventure."

Some people don't want to bathe in salt water or may be in an area where it is too cold. Others share Paula's enthusiasm for ocean bathing. Privacy when bathing is a problem for some cruisers. Modesty is a cultural trait. If there are only two of you on board or yours is the only boat in an anchorage, privacy isn't a problem. In other situations you may have to change habits or attitudes.

We discovered that bathing was the same as washing dishes or clothes in Papeete, Tahiti. All the boats were Med-moored, stern to the quay, packed in like sardines. At about ten o'clock in the morning, our neighbors stripped down and proceeded to shower on deck, all the while carrying on conversations with us, people on shore, and anyone who happened to pass by. We quickly discovered this practice was the norm and followed suit. It was a liberating experience.

Bathing naked on deck or on shore in Annapolis or in a Muslim country might cause an entirely different reaction. We cruised on Lake Huron with a young couple from Switzerland. When they jumped naked into the water to bathe, a nearby boat with five young men startled us by whistling, shouting, and watching them with binoculars. Our friends were not embarrassed, but they wondered what caused the commotion.

On *Nalu IV*, we typically soap up and rinse with salt water, and then we do a final freshwater rinse. With some soap products, you must use a large quantity to make a lather in salt water. If you try to rinse immediately in fresh water, the foaming properties seem to increase and it is nearly impossible to get all the soap off. We do not buy special saltwater soaps or Joy dish detergent. We use the same biodegradable liquid soap for bodies, hair, clothes, and dishes.

For freshwater rinsing, we used to use the black plastic showers that absorb the sunlight during the day to heat water. In the Mediterranean, we discovered that many cruisers use portable garden sprayers. The can holds about three gallons of water, a hand pump pressurizes it, and the sprayer is very efficient for rinsing. To make sure water inside warmed up, we painted our yellow sprayer with black stripes.

Hair Care

When we left on our first long cruise, I had a neighbor come over to teach me how to give myself a permanent. Jim watched carefully, because I told him that I couldn't do the back by myself. Besides, I regularly cut his hair, and this would be his chance to return the favor. Six months later he had his first opportunity to give me a perm.

I carefully wound all the rods for the top and the sides, partitioning the hair, wrapping the ends with paper, and rolling the rods tightly. When it was complete, I gave him the comb, papers, and rods to finish the back. In a matter of minutes, he declared himself done. I was astonished at his speed until I saw the pile of unused papers and curlers. "I didn't need all of those because your hair is so thin," he explained when I questioned doing all of the back of my head on four curling rods.

Barbara Colborn had an adept and cooperative mate. Before they went cruising, her hairdresser showed her husband how to cut her hair. "The first few months it really wasn't very good," she says of her onboard coiffure. "But I told him, 'I want this and that differently,' and we worked on it. . . . He's learning and he's going to get better and better at it."

Not having great success with my husband's haircare services, my solution was to get permanents in foreign countries as I needed them. I became expert on permanents around the world: Australia was no problem; in Djibouti, Africa, the salon was French, the permanent absolutely gorgeous, and it cost $100; in the Balearic Islands, I practiced my Spanish and had good success for about $30; Yugoslavia was undergoing incredible inflation, but I paid $6 and gave the woman who did my hair another $6 as a tip; Switzerland, Barbados, and St. Lucia were all hair successes.

There are other solutions to hair care. Learn to cut your own hair. If you can cut only the front and sides, do that. Let the back grow and pull it into a ponytail or braid. Or locate another cruiser who cuts hair professionally. Without fail, we have found anchorages in the Caribbean and Mexico populated with professionals who do haircuts on their boats or on the beach as a regular business.

One caution for those who have not lived in the sun full time: Sun damages hair just as it damages skin. The result is brittle, dry hair that is bleached and breaks off. Wear a hat and use protective shampoos and conditioners to ward off the ultraviolet rays.

Skin Care and Makeup

I talked about sun protection for the skin in an earlier chapter on health issues.

I myself lost the battle before starting long-term cruising by sailing without wearing sunblock. In northern latitudes, the destructive power of the sun's rays are often discounted because the warm sunshine feels so good. As a result, the damage is done. And there is no wrinkle cream that can improve the situation. Plastic surgery is an option, but the expense and impermanence hardly make it seem worthwhile. I like to believe people when they say that wrinkles give me character.

Even though I can't take back the wrinkles and lines, I try to use a moisturizer with a sun protection factor in it every day. I never can remember to renew sunblocks or zinc oxide, but I do remember to put on moisturizer. Some moisturizers contain a color base or sunblock. Regardless of what you use, it is no good if you forget to apply it.

Protecting the skin is not limited to the face, although we do pay more attention to facial skin. The thin skin on the neck and the backs of hands shows sun damage quickly. Arms and legs have thicker skin, but wrinkles and discoloration eventually catch up. Unless you have no pigment in your skin, you have some tolerance for the ultraviolet rays. The extent to which you expose your skin will ultimately determine your skin condition as you get older.

Makeup is an alternative for skin protection. Most women find makeup unsatisfactory in warm climates because of perspiration and many forego makeup when they cruise. Paula Dinius had no problem once they set out cruising. "It was harder living on the boat when I had a job, because I had to have more toiletries and face the world with hair done and clothes pressed. Once we left to go cruising, my lipstick never came out of the cupboard in five years."

Barbara Colborn, on the other hand, said "I learned that lipstick and earrings go a long way to make you look good when you're wearing T-shirt and pants."

Some women want the finished appearance of makeup and have found ways to make it possible while cruising. I encountered two young women in Australia who had just had their eyelashes and eyebrows dyed. A more extreme measure some women use is tattooing features such as eyebrows.

Each of us has a standard of appearance that we are comfortable with. When Barbara Colborn and her husband went cruising, they agreed on what their standard would be: ". . . we wanted to be like those English adventurers who would go into the jungle in the old movies. You see them shaving, and the women would always have their hair looking clean and tidy. We wanted to make that effort to keep our personal looks together."

Clothing

Barbara Marrett recalls her first reaction to clothing as a cruising issue. "I'm not a real fashion plate so I really enjoyed simplifying my life. You can't take many clothes or much jewelry on a 31-foot boat. Most of the people you meet cruising are not judging you by your looks or what you're wearing, anyway. The more primitive people seem very astute at judging body language to learn who you are, rather than judging you by what you say or wear."

Clothing is still something many women worry about when they go cruising. Wearing only one color for months is unappealing (and unknown to most of us). On land, we have lots of clothing in closets, cabinets, and drawers. But when confronted with a single hanging locker and two or three drawers on a boat for everything you own, it is difficult to imagine how you will manage.

Most women don't limit themselves to items of all one color, although there may be some excellent reasons for that practice. There was a time when navy blue was the only yachting color. The best argument for navy blue is that it doesn't show the dirt; the argument against navy blue is that it is too dark to be worn in hot climates. White was the hot-weather alternative, but cruisers have learned that white is rarely practical when you have to beach a dinghy, carry bags of groceries, or sit on thatched mats for a cold drink.

The space for clothing may be very limited, so you should wear the things you like that make you feel good. Patricia Miller said her wardrobe in Mexico consisted of three swimsuits and two dresses. That may sound unrealistic, but she makes a good point: Clothing should be appropriate for what you do. Sailing and living on the water in a warm climate make swimsuits the preferred item of clothing. Dresses are more comfortable than pants in warm climates. And in Mexico, most women wear dresses rather than pants. If you have to scale down to a limited wardrobe, think about where you will be. Your clothing needs to be appropriate for other cultures. Through experience I learned that in order to gain acceptance as someone more than a tourist in Asia and the Arab world, I had to accept their dress standards.

There are times when you may need something special to wear. Most cruisers manage to pull themselves together for special occasions. Paula Dinius said, "We always had one special outfit to go out. You wear fancier shoes, do your hair, nails, and makeup. You don't have to be raggedy all the time. The guys would dress up and we'd stand in the dinghy so we didn't get wet going ashore."

Lin Pardey describes herself as a non-materialistic person, and she managed very well with limited space. "I have two designer evening gowns, alligator shoes, and belt. When I go out, I dress as well as I wish."

After an absence of nearly seven years, we returned to our home port. We had worn-out swimsuits and underwear, because that was our standard attire on the boat. We still had T-shirts, shorts, pants, sweaters, and shoes that we carried around and didn't wear. We used our dress-up clothes and replaced them once, because they were very worn. Even though we thought we were traveling light, we brought home excess clothes.

The fabric your clothes are made of has much to do with your comfort level. Although many people advocate using synthetics because they are lightweight, warm when necessary, and wrinkle-free, we take the opposite stance. Most synthetic fabrics are too warm for the truly hot climates. Stores in Florida and California don't carry clothes that are warm enough to wear in Minnesota in the winter, and your stores at home are not likely to have fabrics designed for comfort in the tropics. Take along what you have that's appropriate, but leave room to buy something later on.

Sex at Sea

During a seminar break one woman asked, "How do you have sex at sea if one person is on watch and the other one is asleep?" There are many times when both of you are awake and sharing your time. Sex is not something you put off until you get to port. Cruising couples make time for sex. But since you're not going to bed at the same time, you have to develop a different approach to sex.

"Sex is more natural because you are more in your body and less in your head," says Barbara Marrett. "If the sailing is really calm and nice, it flows." Migael Scherer shared Barbara's view of the surrounding environment: "Romance can be cultivated on a boat. On land, there are so many distractions. I think the boat helped us."

The freedom of sex outdoors in the daylight was appealing to some of the women interviewed. "Underway on passages you're out hundreds of miles from people. You have the cockpit, which is wonderful. It doesn't get much more private than that," says Barbara Colborn.

Louise Burke, who lost her sea-going husband but continued on as an offshore sailor, advised: "Become a team. Curl up at night in your new nest and feel confident and sublimely happy at sharing this new adventure with your lover or husband. Remember, a quiet anchorage, a strange harbor, and exotic night noises can bring out the best in the beast."

Cruisers are adventurers, and your sex life can be another area of exploration. Living on a boat, sailing across an ocean, or anchoring in a still cove offers opportunities: from lovemaking to swimming naked in the starlight, trying every bunk cushion on the boat, and slipping away from other people and boats in your dinghy. I find the dinghy is often the best answer because we can get away from the boat, especially when we have crew. At night, we drift under the stars to our hearts' content. We have had couples with us who simply retired early and asked us to turn up the stereo for an hour or so.

One final comment on a story often heard among cruisers: I don't believe it's true that submarines surface when they see a cruiser in the middle of the ocean just to see what's happening in the cockpit.

16

Making
the Most
of It

WHETHER IT IS YOUR FIRST TRIP to the opera and you don't know the story, or you go to Wimbledon without knowing tennis, you may understand the significance of the event, but without the specific knowledge the magic is lost. Cruising is no different. It can be the event of a lifetime. But in order to make the most of it, you need to prepare and educate yourself in advance.

Cruising has many different aspects, and it is hard to know where to begin in your preparations. I learned the hard way when we sailed to Australia via the South Pacific. I had focused on all the necessary tasks before our departure, such as organizing provisions and boat gear. But I neglected to research the places where we would stop during our voyage. When we arrived in French Polynesia, I realized my mistake. I wrote to the States and requested that a guide book and a French-English dictionary be sent out to us.

The books caught up with me in Fiji. Granted, I did see some wonderful sights in Polynesia, but I missed many others. The places I missed are not forgotten: I hope someday to return and have a second chance.

You won't have time to become an expert on everything you see and do, but you can prepare yourself enough to ensure you don't miss the once-in-a-lifetime opportunities.

Things to Learn for Independence

There are two areas you can focus on in advance of your departure that will help you be more independent and, I believe, improve your quality of life as a cruiser: operating the dinghy and speaking the local language.

Dinghy Operation

A friend once complained to me about being at anchor: "I prefer being in the marina. Then I don't have to wait on someone else to go places." When I asked her what she meant, she said, "I can't drive the dinghy, so I'm always stuck."

Learning to drive a dinghy may not seem important to you. But it is no different from not being able to drive a car or ride a bicycle. If you have to wait for someone to chauffeur you ashore and to other boats, then you are not independent.

If you are only cruising on holidays and vacations, going solo in the dinghy may not be important. But if you are going on long cruises and you want to make the early market or powerwalk on the beach at sunrise, being able to get yourself ashore is essential.

My friend chose not to learn how to use the dinghy. Her options were limited and she remained dependent on her mate, or someone else, for transportation when they were not in a marina. The situation was even more critical in areas where marinas don't exist.

If you are going ashore to do chores, sightsee, or handle business, you need to use the dinghy. You'll also need this skill if you want to visit friends, go snorkeling, or explore a lagoon. Using the dinghy should be second nature.

What do you need to know? For me the hardest part of dinghy operation is starting the outboard engine. After seventeen years, I was pushed to the point of insisting our outboard be replaced. Even when I got it started, which was rare, it would run briefly and die. Jim was having the same difficulties, and we agreed it was time for a new engine. The outboard we have now is easy to start and quieter to operate, and it has safety features our old engine didn't have.

Starting an outboard is a simple procedure. Read the instruction manual for the basics. Practice starting and driving. Learn to recognize if you have flooded the engine, which will prevent it from starting. Newer engines with pull starters are much easier to operate than older models.

Even though our newer model is better behaved, we still invoke the following as dinghy drivers: Please God, look with kindness on this poor sinner and these two cylinders.

The first time I went off alone in our dinghy, I realized I could start it, stop it, and beach it. But I had never learned to pull alongside a dock or other boats. Fortunately, our dinghy is a rubber inflatable one, and it bounces off other dinghies, docks, and our boat. I got a few jolts—and some unpleasant commentary—but I didn't do any damage to others, myself, or the dinghy.

If you don't want to operate an outboard engine, learn to row the dinghy unassisted. Be sure that the oars, oarlocks, and seat accommodate you. It is easier to row a hard dinghy, which is designed to be rowed, than it is to row an inflatable one. Many boats have two dinghies, the same way families have two cars. It's a good idea if you have the space to stow them.

Speaking the Language

A second way to increase your independence is with language skills. Being fluent in the language of your cruising venue isn't absolutely necessary, but having some facility with the language will enhance your enjoyment. English is spoken worldwide, and you can make yourself understood. But you cannot converse freely with the local inhabitants.

If you studied a language in school, brush up on it. Spanish and French are both valuable languages for cruising in the Western Hemisphere. Mexico, Central America, and South America (except Brazil) are Spanish-speaking countries. French is spoken on the Caribbean islands of Martinique, Guadeloupe, and St. Martin.

Acquire a basic understanding of grammar and pronunciation of a language before you go cruising. As you sail from place to place, you can acquire the vocabulary you need. Everyday tasks, such as shopping or going to the post office, are good times to practice a language. You need to learn how to count, ask for prices, and learn simple phrases of greeting and appreciation.

The rewards may be respect from the locals or freedom to travel off the beaten path, try out new places and new foods, and make new friends. There is some security in knowing you can ask questions and get answers. Language will expand your world.

Grow As You Go

In the throes of planning for your departure, there is much to accomplish. You have to put some things on hold, but those things need not be forgotten altogether. You can work time into your cruising schedule for those endeavors once you are sailing.

"Dream up a list of five fun, rewarding, enriching, and absorbing activities, mental and physical, that you've always wanted to do in your spare time," recommends Patricia Miller. "Adapt them to boat life . . . one at a time. Weave time for this activity into your daily routine and let it become a new habit. By the time you've completed this list, you'll have become a more interesting and organized person, and you'll already have dreamed up a new list." Those activities may include sewing, dancing, collecting shells, photography, and more.

Patricia discourages including things on that list involved with boat maintenance, such as varnishing. I agree to some degree, but I also know some women who love to varnish. They take pride in their work, which is better than anything a boatyard might do. The things you learn should be things you want to do for your own pleasure and satisfaction.

Cruising Skills

With the advancements in onboard electronic instruments, navigation today has been reduced to pushing buttons and reading dimly lit screens. Your cruising partner may be, like my husband, a nut about gadgets. Still, learning to navigate the old-fashioned way, by using a sextant, is essential.

Once you learn, however, your skills can get rusty unless you use them. We make a point of using our sextant periodically to keep our skills sharp. Plotting your course on a chart is another skill that gets ignored, and it's easy to get sloppy if you don't do it regularly.

I find plotting our positions on a chart and following our progress an absorbing activity during a passage. The geography-class explanation of latitude and longitude we all learned in school didn't have much meaning. But taking the latitude/longitude position from a sextant, or from electronics such as a SatNav or GPS, and putting it on a chart gives me a picture of where we are. Some women have sailed with us for hundreds of miles and never bothered to look at a chart. My curiosity would drive me crazy if I didn't know our position and course.

When we swap charts with friends, I like to match position plots to see if we sailed the same course and if we took the same amount of time. Notations written on their chart of what they saw—such as "Whales!" or "Caught fish!"—alert us to new activities.

The plotting activity has true value. Electronic devices can quit. But on your chart is a record of where you are. It is a safety net and valuable knowledge to have while you are working to get your electronic gear back online or dig out your sextant. If you are coastal cruising, plotting your course to avoid obstructions such as shoals and rocks is essential.

Learning to use a radio may not be something you have time to do before you go cruising. The VHF and single-sideband (SSB) radios only require you to have the Federal Communications Commission (FCC) ship's station license in order to use them. After you make local contact with marinas and other boats on a VHF, you may be interested in reaching contacts farther away on the SSB.

If you enjoy learning radio procedures and regulations, you might consider getting your amateur radio operator's license (ham) so that you can participate in nets and have virtually unlimited communication. As you learn Morse code and regulations, you progress through different levels, acquiring more privileges and broadening your horizons on more frequencies. Write to the FCC in Gettysburg, Pennsylvania, for information on getting a ham license, or contact the American Radio Relay League in Newington, Connecticut, for information on classes and local resources.

Some women are attracted to learning the mechanical skills needed to keep various boat systems operational. Lin Pardey was the exception to the rule thirty years ago when she started cruising. "I liked the mechanics of sailing. I'm quite a mechanical person and I like to know how the boat works," she says. "Just being around boats and understanding how they work, I found that men treated me special. It was a male-oriented world."

The basics of engine operation and maintenance may seem unfamiliar, but they are not complicated. Checking the oil, the coolant, the transmission fluid, and the zincs is often more easily done by a woman than a man.

Barbara Colborn had thought of the engine as a black hole, but she learned it was more than that. "I'm gradually learning more about the engine through doing simple maintenance. Mechanics is like cooking. I wrote out the directions for changing the oil like a recipe: You gather up your tools, then you do step one, step two, step three. Women have smaller hands generally, and they can get in there very easily and do things quickly."

In the past, women had to fight stereotypes in order to do mechanical things. Today, women learn mechanical and electrical skills; many find those mechanical skills fun, enriching, and useful.

I rarely do the oil change, but I still do regular checks of engine fluids and battery condition, and I keep maintenance records.

Personal Skills

After you start cruising, you discover skills you never knew existed to add to your list of things to learn.

A talented young man crewed for us on a passage to Tahiti. He played the guitar, banjo, harmonica, and five-penny whistle. During an evening's entertainment, he taught me to play the spoons. I would have never put that skill on a list, yet it proved to be fun and a good way to participate in impromptu musicales. I went so far as to have wooden spoons made by a Marquesan wood carver to create a new type of sound.

Musical instruments are always important for entertainment. Even when you can't speak a local language, the ability to play an instrument will break the ice and be your entree to local activities. You can practice acoustical and portable electronic instruments on an ocean passage and play them on arrival.

Other forms of entertainment, particularly ones children enjoy, can be a great introduction to a new island or village.

We carry a variety of hand puppets on board that we have acquired over the years. On the quay in Manihi in the Tuamotu Archipelago, children gathered to watch the captain smoke his pipe. A raccoon puppet named Porky poked his head through a port to mimic the captain. The captain scolded, and we were suddenly in the midst of a Punch and Judy show. The children were delighted. The only downside was that about thirty children arrived on the quay at sunrise the next day chanting "Porky, Porky, Porky."

Simple arts-and-crafts projects make great gifts and increase your enjoyment of cruising. Collecting seeds, nuts, and shells is popular. You can create something to wear or decorate your boat with your collection.

Acquiring things as you cruise is easy. Knowing what to do with them so they are useful and justify the space they occupy on board is difficult. Photography, sketching, and painting help you remember beautiful places and recapture memories. These activities also satisfy the need to do something creative and enriching.

Not all of us want to collect or create, and not all of us are inclined to perform. The one activity in which most cruisers indulge is reading. We've read hundreds of paperbacks and traded them for more. For a while, we read without any particular goal in mind. But we developed the need to have a library that would provide information about our destinations.

At first we read the standard travel guides for basic information about ground transportation, holidays, money exchange, and sightseeing. We discovered a need to have a better understanding of some places and began reading more history. One of the most memorable books was David McCullough's *Path Between the Seas,* which is the story of the building of the Panama Canal. It gave the trip through the Canal more significance because we knew the human cost of the project.

Popular fiction with sound historical research, such as James

Michener's *Mexico*, provides historical and cultural information with good entertainment. And don't forget to put a good atlas and encyclopedia aboard to use for reference.

If you enjoy writing but don't want to worry about deadlines and contracts, write for your own pleasure. You might even develop a newsletter for friends and family eager to share in your adventures. Make and send copies, or send your original copy home and ask someone to copy and distribute it for you.

Smell the Roses

"Herb likes to sail and I like to get someplace," says Nancy Payson. "I enjoy being there and walking, hiking, meeting the locals, getting to know the culture. Herb's an 'A to B-er,' but I make him slow down and smell the roses as we go along." Nancy and Barbara Marrett agree that for many women, the attraction to cruising is the travel.

Unless you are trying to set a record for speed or for the highest number of places visited on a cruise, spend time in your destinations. Travel the way the local people do—be it on foot, in trucks, on horses, or on camels. Attend the local church or festival to learn more about the people and their culture. Take along a camera and a tape recorder (if it doesn't offend people). A great way to learn about a country and its people is to get on a local bus and ride to the end of the line. If trains are the standard way to travel, pack a lunch, a water bottle, and tissues, and get on a train for the day.

We have found trains a fascinating way to travel. In New Zealand, the very old trains didn't have dining cars or toilets, so we stopped regularly at little country stations to sample terrific home cooking and use the facilities. In Sri Lanka, the train was so crowded that we sat in the vestibule on our sea bags. On the slow-moving train, we felt like characters in an old English movie. The Karanda train in Australia was like an amusement park ride; the track twisted into the mountains past waterfalls, brilliant plants, and wild animals.

Don't wear a watch. Leave your schedule on the boat and sample something new. Let the days flow at their own pace.

A friend of mine often says, "You only go around once. But if you do it right, once should be enough."

17

A Few
Words About
Provisioning

FIFTEEN YEARS AGO, it was common for cruisers to set out for foreign waters carrying food and supplies for six months. In some of the less-traveled parts of the world today, such as the Red Sea, there still is trepidation about the availability of provisions. But when you set off on a passage, I think you will be surprised by your discoveries: You may not find your favorite granola in every port, but you will find good basic food.

Provisioning for Cruising

When I started daysailing, provisions were simple: soup, sandwiches, cookies, apples, coffee, and toilet paper. As I progressed to weekend cruising, so did the food on board. I would make turkey dinners and Eggs Benedict (to name only two dishes), seal the meals in boilable bags, freeze them, then reheat them on board in boiling water. I didn't have a refrigerator, but, for a weekend, food kept fine in a picnic cooler.

Provisioning for my first weeklong excursion was more complicated. But we anchored each night within reach of little country stores, and I had plenty of fresh food and staples.

The first offshore passage I provisioned for was a race from Los Angeles to Honolulu called the TransPacific Yacht Race. The racing rules required that I submit a complete menu for twenty-one days, plus a listing of five days' emergency rations. Not only was I required to provision for three weeks, I was doing it for a crew of eight!

It took me nearly two days to write out a complete menu for the race. I considered the cooking skills of the crew: seven men, aged eighteen to fifty, and me. They all were expected to cook and do dishes, just as I was expected to steer and trim sails. I didn't have storage for leftovers, and refrigeration space was limited on board. I developed a grocery list from my menu, accounting for everything down to the last candy bar. By now I have had lots of practice, and I still write detailed menus for passages of more than five hundred miles. If I plan off the top of my head as I shop, I am likely to forget a necessary ingredient. But with a written list, I can remind myself to get the ingredients for fun items, too: birthday cake, popcorn, and our special favorite—ice cream.

For me, planning menus down to the last jar of mushrooms is still the easiest way to manage provisioning. This planning may be the antithesis of the cruiser's credo of going where the wind takes you. But it is a way to learn.

Start by discussing the type of weather and sea conditions you are likely to have and estimate the number of days you will be at sea. If you average one hundred miles a day, and you are doing a three-hundred-mile passage, plan on three days plus one more. If you make it in three days, you have extra food on board for an unforeseen delay, such as a slow clearance into port. If you don't make your one-hundred-mile days, you will have sufficient food.

Keep things simple for meals underway. Planning to do meals with many different side dishes when you are going to weather is an acrobatic feat. Food for a passage needs to be easy to prepare, attractive, fresh, and hot. Stick with familiar meals: Experimenting with a new dish while underway is courting disaster.

The first day on a passage, I make mild food so no one starts out with indigestion, which might lead to seasickness. Chicken with rice, porcupine meatballs, or pasta are easily prepared in one pot. Served with bread and sliced fresh fruit, they make substantial meals that are easy to fix and eat.

I know one woman whose planning is excellent. She makes sure there are leftovers from the evening meal, then makes them the foundation for lunch the next day. Leftover chicken and rice can become soup; pasta can be used to make a salad; meatballs might be sandwich filling. The refrigerator doesn't fill up with leftovers, and lunch is something other than sandwiches.

Some believe that a planned-menu approach to provisioning does not leave any room for flexibility, but putting something in writing doesn't mean you can't change it. If the weather is too warm for hot soup, make cold soup. Or swap meals for something more appropriate. The reason for thorough menu planning is to guarantee you have all the provisions you need.

Even though I plan my menus, I like the flexibility of substituting a freshly caught mahi-mahi for, say, meatballs.

You can't plan on finding fresh fish along the way, so when you do, juggle a little. I store fresh food so the most perishable items will be used first, and I can see what I am supposed to use next. If fresh fish is plentiful, cook perishable menu ingredients so they won't spoil. Then find another way to use the meal.

When gunkholing, I generally carry enough fresh food for three days. I trust our ability to locate a grocery store, friendly locals who have goods to sell, or fresh food from the environment. The plan has not failed me yet: I have never had to depend on fish, coconuts, or berries from the wild as a main source of food.

Shopping in Foreign Countries

Shopping is one of the most entertaining and educational experiences you have as a cruiser. Whether you are in a new town or a new country, food is a common denominator that helps you get acquainted with the local people and learn about the area.

Remember, in some ports you will have to translate your shopping list into a foreign language. Learning to count verbally is important— although you can always use your fingers. Knowing how to say thank you is an essential part of your language lesson.

You will also have to do measurement translations. Metric measure is used in most of the world outside the United States. You will have to translate to kilos and grams in your recipes. My shortcuts for conversion are: a half-kilogram is slightly more than a pound; a liter is a touch more than a quart. Use a small pocket calculator to convert measurements, track spending, and convert currency.

For me, the first shopping excursion sets the tone for the rest of our stay. I learn about the people, their food, and their attitude toward me. I make every effort to put my best foot forward. I dress the same way as the local people: If the women wear skirts and cover their heads, I do too. I still may look different, but I try to avoid calling undue attention to myself.

The first shopping run also gives me the opportunity to judge prices and availability—in case we need to do a major provisioning before we leave—and to learn the local market hours. In much of the world, shopping is done early in the day. It is not unusual for markets to open at 6:00 A.M. If you wait until too late in the day, the stalls will be closed or the shelves empty.

I also learn what kinds of extra containers I might need for my next trip. In some places, you need your own bottles and jars for oil, vinegar, honey, jam, and wine. For items such as beer and yogurt, there may be a deposit on the containers.

In most countries, the shopping bags are plastic. So wherever I shop—even in the United States—I bring my own bags and baskets to carry purchases. Disposing of plastic is a problem; it makes better sense not to accumulate it in the first place.

I have learned to bring specialized containers to market. I have plastic egg cartons, because eggs are often sold in open flats or loose in a basket. I have a long canvas bag lined with plastic to keep bread fresh and protect it from spray on the dinghy ride back. A string bag is great for fruits and vegetables.

On major provisioning trips, my own containers are not enough. I resort to paper boxes or wooden crates. Try to avoid bringing those local containers on board, since they may contain cockroaches. Dispose of paper wrappers, such as those on flour sacks or cereal containers. If they have been on the shelf for a long time, they might house nests for insect eggs.

The other part of my shopping excursion is to check the availability and quality of water, as well as sources for propane.

After shopping, I have to get my goods back to the boat. Taxis, buses, bikes, and feet work fine if we're on a dock. Many cruisers use fold-up carts to manage heavy items, such as sodas and beer. I have both owned and rented motor scooters in various ports, and I find them ideal. A large plastic box wired on the back generally handles all that I want to carry.

If we are at anchor, the dinghy is the final mode of transportation to the boat. I like a big dinghy, since it carries people, provisions, water, and fuel—sometimes all at once. If you have any distance to go from shore to the boat, think in terms of a dinghy that will be capable of doing all the chores in one or two trips. Otherwise, you may be running back and forth when you could be snorkeling, sightseeing, or loafing.

What's Out There

Whether you are passagemaking or gunkholing, your menu needs to reflect what you will be able to buy when you go ashore. The eating habits of the local population reflect what is readily available and appropriate for the climate.

Basic staples are available everywhere: sugar, flour, baking powder, salt, oil, beans, rice, and green coffee beans. I buy these items automatically every month, along with toilet paper, paper towels, soap, bleach, and matches. We can store these comfortably. Canned goods available around the world include fish, fruit, tomato sauce or puree, and beans.

Produce in the tropics is heavy on fruit—including mangoes, papayas, bananas, pineapples, guavas, and citrus. Peppers, tomatoes, onions, and squash are common. It is harder to find good potatoes, green vegetables, lettuce, carrots, and cabbage, because they grow in cooler temperatures. Tropical countries with high mountains offer a broader range of food.

Fresh dairy and meat products are harder to find in the tropics. Animals are not prevalent and refrigeration not common. Yogurt from sheep's, goat's, or cow's milk can be found in many small towns and villages. Fish, in one form or another, seems to be available anywhere you cruise.

We have found that bacon, salami, and ham are rarely available in Islamic countries. Beer, wine, and liquor are hard to find in the Arab countries; in Sudan, for instance, religious laws are enforced by the government, and no liquor is available.

Countries at latitudes similar to my home port's have had the same foods. In Europe—including Yugoslavia, Turkey, and Greece—the problem was not availability, it was deciding what I wanted!

Many women are concerned about the quality of food, but I rarely find that to be a problem. Sometimes the inventory in a small store is depleted or the packaging damaged. I have learned to ask for things, because there may be inventory in storage. If a store is out of bread or produce, ask when the next delivery is expected.

It's hard to find tender meat or chicken in countries where animals are eaten only after their productive years. The pressure cooker is great for making tender beef and chicken. Lack of refrigeration in some countries means you must select live animals. Usually, they are butchered and prepared according to your instructions. I usually select the animals first, do my shopping, and return for the meat last.

If you never learned how to cut up chickens or what parts of animals yield roast, chops, or steaks, keep an old cookbook, such as a 1950s *Betty Crocker's Picture Cookbook*, in your cruising library. I keep a cleaver for such tasks. I also use a food processor to make my own ground meats.

Lura Francis canned meat on board her Westsail 32 when she was in

Cyprus. She follows a low-salt diet, and commercially canned meat is loaded with salt. Plus, she says her canned meat tasted great. She stowed the pint jars, separated by strips of bubble wrap, in lockers beneath the ship's bunks. During a six-year circumnavigation, Lura experienced heavy weather, including a hurricane, but never found a broken jar.

We regularly use certain spices and condiments in our menus. I try to always keep those items on hand. When I find one of our favorites in an unlikely place, I buy it and tuck it away. These items include peanuts, capers, olives, pimento, chutney, pickle relish, raisins, wine vinegar, bottled lemon juice, Worcestershire sauce, Dijon mustard, olive oil, tarragon, basil, cumin, corn starch, brown sugar, vanilla, oatmeal, popcorn, and honey.

Foreign Finds

Cruising in countries without freezers, microwaves, and pre-packaged meals opens up new opportunities. The lack of what we call convenience foods is replaced by food products that are ideal for the cruiser.

Ultra–heat treated (UHT) milk is treated with heat so it can be kept without refrigeration for six months. It is common throughout the world, and it is available as whole, skim, and partially skim milk in liter boxes. I had more difficulty finding box milk in the United States than in any other country.

One spin-off product I found, and use a great deal, is cream in a box. I have used a 250-milliliter box of whipping cream to make ice cream. "Anchor" brand, made in New Zealand, is available in many countries.

Canned butter is occasionally found in the United States (and nearly everywhere else). Both Holland and New Zealand produce excellent canned butter. Other canned products I have found in the South Pacific, Australia, Asia, and Europe include cheese, bacon, ham, beef, hot dogs, and whole chickens. In the United States, our microwaves and freezers have made many canned goods obsolete.

I found dried vegetables in Australia. These were dehydrated, not freeze-dried. When reconstituted in cooking, they tasted like fresh vegetables. Varieties included peas, string beans, peas with carrots, and peas with corn. I stocked up on those vegetables before I left Australia, but I wasn't able to find them in Asia, Africa, Europe, or the Americas.

A relatively new item in Mexico is shredded, dried meat. It can be kept on the shelf, just like the dried vegetables. I use it for spaghetti sauce, chili, and stew.

Prepackaged mixes and convenience foods common in American

supermarkets are becoming more available in other parts of the world. There are biscuit mixes, pancake mixes, and cookie mixes similar to American products. The drawback for me is cost; items imported from the States, or made to appeal to a small portion of the population, are expensive. Consequently, I do without or make substitutes. With experimentation I have learned to make biscuit mix, instant hot chocolate mix, pie crust mix, peanut butter, and more.

The one item I have missed and found no real substitute for is American pickle relish. In Australia, I bought something that looked like the slime from a fish tank. It was tasteless. In some parts of Mexico, I found jars of pickle relish that looked as if they had been on the shelf since the time of Zapata. As a result, everyone who comes to visit us brings pickle relish.

Bright Copper Kettles

My prize possession is a copper teakettle with a fast-heating coil in the bottom. I don't recommend copper for everyone, but I do recommend equipping your galley with certain pots that work in every galley—large or small.

The most frequently used is the teakettle. Many cruisers prefer to boil water in a sauce pan, but the teakettle is safer—if it spills or falls off the stove, the contents are less likely to scald bystanders. In addition, less heat and moisture escape into the atmosphere.

I find a pressure cooker the most valuable pot in the galley. The modern pressure cooker is quite safe, performs a variety of functions, and is ideal for cooking one-pot meals. Select a pressure cooker of at least four-quart capacity; unless you have a huge crew or plan to do canning, there is no need for a giant cooker. I prefer stainless steel—it is easy to maintain, particularly with saltwater washing. The rubber seals will deteriorate in the saltwater environment, so be sure to buy spares. Most pressure cookers come with instruction booklets and recipes. Practice with the unit before you leave home so you are comfortable with its basic functions. You can learn to cook nearly anything in a pressure cooker, including bread.

Another basic pot is a deep skillet (or sauteuse). In a kitchen you might use a skillet or crepe pan for doing a variety of chores, from frying eggs to sautéing fish. Those same chores can be done in a similar pan at sea, but the pan should have higher sides.

Stainless steel equipment is great, because it is easy to clean and does not corrode. If you have aluminum, there is no reason to throw it out until it is worn out. In a saltwater environment, it takes more effort to keep aluminum from corroding. Iron kettles and pots rust too quickly for my taste, so I don't keep them on board. Enameled iron is very nice, until the enamel chips.

I believe in having one good thermal bottle on board. I can heat water, coffee, soup, or a variety of liquids and keep them hot in a thermal bottle without using fuel to reheat liquids. Night watches and rough weather are more tolerable with a cup of something hot. Cold beverages can also be made in a thermal bottle and kept cold in hot climates. It is important to buy a first-quality bottle to assure getting the best insulation.

I also have a griddle in my galley. This may seem redundant with a deep skillet on board, but a griddle can be used for french toast, pancakes, or grilled cheese sandwiches, and its primary value is its efficiency. My griddle covers two burners and can accommodate ten slices of french toast or six chops. When you have a hungry crowd aboard, the griddle is a lifesaver.

Space is always a consideration, so I try to have pots and pans that nest inside each other. The same rule applies to oven pans, if you have an oven.

Be careful when choosing oven pans. Boat stoves have small ovens, and oven size will restrict your choices when you buy pans. Measure your oven interior carefully before buying equipment. I make lots of pizza on board. I was often tempted to buy a pizza pan, but the diameter of a standard pizza pan is an inch too big for my oven. I make rectangular pizzas instead.

I store sharp knives in a knife block screwed down to the counter; the knives can be latched in bad weather. Never leave knives on a counter, because they will fly off with the least provocation. I store all other utensils in a drawer accessible to the stove.

The utensils in the galley are the same ones you use in your kitchen, except they are made of stainless steel: spatulas, can openers, tongs, graters, measuring spoons, cups, etc. Plastic and wooden utensils are great, although less sturdy. My measuring utensils are both English and metric, to match my varied cookbooks.

The standard home appliances I used as a liveaboard—blender, mixer, coffee maker, toaster, microwave—may not be practical on some boats. If you can generate the electricity to operate these appliances and keep them from rusting, that's fine. But if you are like many cruisers, you need to find reasonable substitutes.

I whip egg whites or cream with a wire whisk. I make toast in the oven or on the griddle. My stainless steel drip coffee pot works fine on the stove. I have used a plastic jar with a snug-fitting lid and lots of arm motion to approximate a blender, although I now have a real blender that operates on 110 volts.

My two concessions are a coffee grinder and a food processor. I roast and grind my own coffee beans. I enjoy real coffee at breakfast, and this is my way of having it every day. My backup is a hand grinder, in case the batteries are down. My food processor gets lots of use if I'm in a marina. Underway, I use it to make bread. It takes three minutes to make and knead dough. The dough rises in a zip-top bag and goes directly to the bread pans for final rise and bake. This system permits me to make fresh bread, even in the roughest conditions, without a big mess.

If you take electric appliances to use when you are plugged into shore power, remember that most of the world operates on 220 volts, 50 cycles. Once you leave the Western Hemisphere you will need a converter.

Tableware

For years I have used Corelle plates and cups. For variety, I have begun adding dinner plates of local handcrafted pottery. Stainless steel is our material of choice for soup bowls, wine glasses, and flatware. I had stainless tumblers, but I replaced them with plastic; ice cubes melted rapidly in hot climates, and in cold climates the cups were uncomfortable to hold when filled with hot beverages. We have a pair of stainless thermal mugs that are all-purpose containers during watches.

Plastic dishes are practical on board, but they have two drawbacks: They cannot be preheated to a high temperature, and the surfaces show scratches after time. If you can find plastic that does not have these problems, let us know!

Our stainless flatware is easy to maintain. It is rugged and still looks good. The only problem I have is the occasional loss of pieces when one is tossed overboard by accident, either with leftovers or in a bucket of saltwater dishwater.

I use cloth napkins and placemats rather than disposable ones. Crew napkins, identified with different colored napkin rings, are used for several days before they are washed. (I tell everyone that I boil the napkins once a week to make soup.) I like cloth because it is more attractive, requires less stowage space than disposable goods, is cheaper to maintain, and does not create garbage.

Stowage

Perishables should be refrigerated. But the definition of a perishable depends on where you shop. If you purchase fresh produce and eggs, they stay fresh for a number of days without refrigeration. Those same items from a supermarket have been in cold storage and will not last unless maintained in the same conditions. Whenever you are concerned about the longevity of an item, purchase it from the source rather than from a store.

Eggs are a classic example. Fresh eggs straight from the chicken can be stored with a light coat of Vaseline and turned over every couple of days for a month. This permits you to store eggs in a drawer, locker, or bilge rather than use precious space in the refrigerator.

Until I reached tropical waters, I used our bilges for storing perishables such as margarine and cheese. The water temperature against the hull made the bilges cool enough to keep these items. When the water temperature climbed above 65°F (18°C), I bought less, stored it in the refrigerator, and used it up in a short space of time.

Handle stowed items in a refrigerator the same way you would at home; the only difference is a top-loading refrigerator will be colder on the bottom, and items that need the coldest temperature should be kept at the bottom. Remember, however, that each time you add items to the refrigerator, they raise the temperature until the box cools down again. Frequent changes in temperature will ruin some items rapidly (for example, dairy products).

You can keep a separate box, such as a picnic cooler, in hot climates for drinks and snacks. If you have frozen food, you can put it in the cooler to defrost.

Mixing unlike items together is a basic mistake in food stowage. The traditional fruit bowl—with bananas, grapes, oranges—looks terrific. But it is rot in the making. You can put lemons, oranges and grapefruit together, but adding the bananas or apples can cost you the whole bunch. When you store items such as potatoes, onions, carrots, beets, and turnips, separate them to prevent contact.

I have seen many cruising boats with net slings used for food stowage. This is a good method of storage, because air can circulate around the items. Some things, such as potatoes, should be kept in the dark to prevent premature sprouting. You can hang a sling in a lazarette.

Plastic containers in your lockers for staples allow you to get rid of paper containers, which can carry roach eggs and get "mushy" in the saltwater environment. You may want to invest in matching Tupperware. I use various plastic containers that I acquire as I travel. Many items are packaged in plastic jars, and they worked just fine to keep out moisture and prevent bug infestation.

Bugs are a problem. Try keeping bugs off the boat. Because cockroaches live in paper boxes and bags, I unload everything in the dinghy and do not bring the sacks or boxes aboard. If I suspect that staples have weevils, I use bay leaves to keep the inhabitants from moving into other inventory. Bombing the boat with an insecticide may be one solution. One woman suggested I winter in an arctic climate to get rid of bugs, but that approach was too extreme for us. Several women recommended "roach hotels" and others use boric acid.

The biggest stowage problem is garbage. There are international rules regarding the disposal of garbage, and it is necessary to abide by them. Even so, a long passage can present real problems.

The best way to avoid the disposal problem is to not have trash. If you can avoid the "overpackaging" that is part of the modern world, then you will not have to be concerned about plastic, foam, and all the rest of the garbage that pollutes the world. Putting the items into other containers and disposing of the wrappers before you leave the dock is the best solution. You may not be able to get rid of all of the packaging, but you can reduce it substantially.

Meat, fruit, and other supermarket staples come in foam trays with plastic covering, and I transfer those items to resealable plastic bags. I use the bags over and over again. If I cannot get rid of the foam trays, I use them for other purposes, such as snack servers. I rinse them in salt water and hang them with clothespins to a lifeline so they can be reused and disposed of at the next port.

You can dispose of biodegradable garbage overboard. Specific rules under the MARPOL Treaty state what can and cannot be discarded at set distances from land. The plaque specifying those limits should be prominently displayed on your boat. There is no place where it is acceptable to dispose of plastic-based materials.

I flatten and break down non-biodegradable garbage and stow it in plastic bags that are tied shut. When sailing between uninhabited places, I burn this type of trash on shore below the high tide line and then bury it. Be sure to remain upwind of fires with plastic and foams in them.

In most countries, the shoreside garbage container is ultimately dumped into the water, which is a very frustrating experience. If you can avoid acquiring trash-making materials, your life will be much easier.

Epilogue

The Voyage Continues

W hen cruisers return from voyages, they may be at a point where they want a different boat, more creature comforts, or more time ashore. Deep down, most of them share an addiction to living an unfettered and simple life. Their voyage may be at an end, but they can hardly wait to get underway again.

I have found that many cruisers have difficulty returning after being away for more than a year. They no longer fit into the community they once called home.

If I am gone for a short period of time, I stay in touch with friends, neighbors, business connections, and social contacts. Few things change in my absence. And a cruise of a few weeks or months is less likely to take me to isolated and unfamiliar places that challenge my value system.

Some women are able to circumnavigate while still returning at regular intervals so they don't lose touch with their communities.

Patricia Miller and Irene Hampshire, both professionals in yacht services, make trips of several months' duration and return to a home-base to care for family, continue jobs, and raise children.

"If you go for a year, you can come home again," says Lin Pardey. "More than two years, you can't come home again. You will have changed and your community will have changed."

After a lengthy absence of two or more years, returning is indeed hard. Going back to the same place, the same house, the same friends, and the same job after a sustained absence is a tough adjustment. For some of us, it is impossible.

Even if a cruise is interrupted for a necessary trip home — because you are over budget, have a family emergency, or develop health problems — friends and family can seem oddly aloof. Time and distance have made them strangers.

Several solutions to this problem have been suggested. Lin recommends, "Come back someplace else. You can rent in a new location or buy a place in a new town. . . . Come back and start over."

When we tried returning to our home port after seven years, it had changed. We were greeted with the question, "When are you moving ashore?" Our joint response was, "We aren't."

Like many other cruisers, the first long voyage had simply whetted our appetite for another one. But our friends at home had assumed that we had seen everything, done everything, and been everywhere we wanted to go. To them, our trip was a mountain to be climbed. Once we scaled to the summit, we would return to normalcy.

Friends saw our life on the boat as hard, fearful, exciting, and inspiring. Still, they expected us to rejoin them in their world. We couldn't fit. We had changed. We no longer had the common ground to keep those friendships going.

Our friends became all the people out on boats around the world. Our mailbox was a stamp collector's dream, filled with letters from everywhere telling us what we were missing. Our boat became a floating boardinghouse for earthbound cruisers passing through. We worked hard for three years so we could finally set out again.

We don't have a homebase. Everything we own is on our boat because our boat is home — our real home. It's comfortable, and it suits us. We talk about what we will do when we get old, but we haven't made a firm plan. There is still too much for us to see and do.

I believe each of us chooses what we want to do with our lives. Even going along without making a conscious choice is a way of choosing.

People who choose to cruise make a commitment to do something they believe will be more fulfilling, more satisfying, more fun, and more rewarding than anything else they can do with their lives. Those are the reasons why cruising is the choice I made.

Appendix

Resources for Cruising Services and Information

Associations/Sailing

National Women's Sailing
Association (NWSA)
Doris Colgate, President
16731 McGregor Boulevard
Ft. Myers, FL 33908
Phone:800-566-NWSA (6972)
941-454-0053
Fax: 941-454-1191

U.S. Sailing Association
PO Box 1260
15 Maritime Drive
Portsmouth, RI 02871-6015
Phone: 401-683-0800
Fax: 401-683-0840

Ham Radio Contacts

American Radio Relay
League (ARRL)
225 Main Street
Newington, CT 06111-1494
Phone: 860-594-0200

Federal Communications
Commission (FCC)
1270 Fairfield Road
Gettysburg, PA 17325-7245
Phone: 800-322-1117
Fax: 717-338-2694

Health Insurance/ Health Agencies

Centers for Disease Control
1600 Clifton Road, NE
Atlanta, GA 30333
Phone: 404-639-3311 (general
administration)
404-332-4559 (International
Travelers' Information
Hotline)

International Health
Insurance danmark a/s
8 Palaegade
1261 Copenhagen K
Denmark
Phone: (45) 33 15 30 99
Fax: (45) 33 32 25 60

Medical Advisory Systems
8050 Southern Maryland
Boulevard
Owings, MD 20736
Phone: 410-257-9505
301-855-8070
Fax: 410-257-2704

PPP Healthcare Group
(Private Patients Plan)
International Insurance
Department
Phillips House
Crescent Road
Tunbridge Wells, Kent
TN1 1BJ
England
Phone: (44) 1892 512345
Fax: (44) 1892 515143

Immunization/Health Requirements

U.S. Government Printing
Office
Attn: Superintendent of
Documents
710 North Capital Street NW
Washington, D.C. 20402
Phone: 202-512-0000 (general
administration)
202-512-1800
(order department)

Home-Study Courses

The Calvert School
105 Tuscany Road
Baltimore, MD 21210
Phone: 410-243-6030

Department of Independent
Study
Brigham Young University
PO Box 21514
206 Harman Building
Provo, UT 84602-1514
Phone: 801-378-2868

Marine Surveyor Information

The National Association of
Marine Surveyors
(NAMS)
PO Box 9306
Chesapeake VA 23321-9306
Phone: 800-822-6267
757-488-9538

Society of Accredited Marine
Surveyors (SAMS)
4162 Oxford Avenue
Jacksonville, FL 32210
Phone: 800-344-9077
904-384-1494
Fax: 904-388-3958

"Be Your Own Sailboat
Surveyor, Almost" (video)
James C. Jessie, Cruiser
Education
Video Learning Library
15838 North 62nd Street
Scottsdale, AZ 85254-1988
Phone: 800-383-8811,
Extension 187
602-596-9970

Sailing Women's Newsletters

*Sister Sail, A Newsletter for
Cruising Women*
Susan Straubing, Editor
PO Box 613
Camden, ME 04843
Phone: 207-236-9498
Fax: 207-236-9691
e-mail: sstraubin@aol.com

*Women Aboard, A Liveaboard
Newsletter*
Maria Russell, Editor
1000 Water Street, S.W. #14
Washington, DC 20024
Phone: 202-484-9171

Sailing Schools/Instruction

Cruising World/US Sailing
Safety-at-Sea Seminars
US Sailing
PO Box 1260
15 Maritime Drive
Portsmouth, RI 02871-6015
Phone: 401-683-0800
Fax: 401-683-0840

Offshore Sailing School
Doris Colgate, President
16731 McGregor Boulevard
Fort Myers, FL 33908
Phone: 800-221-4326
941-454-1700
Fax: 941-454-1191

Seaskills
Pat Clark, Co-owner
37 Geneva Road
Norwalk CT 06850
Phone: 203-838-9014
-and-
Peg Nelson, Co-owner
29 King Street
Apartment 2H
New York, NY 10014
Phone: 212-807-6325

Sea Sense
Carol Cuddyer, President
25 Thames St.
New London, CT 06320
Phone: 800-332-1404
860-444-1404

Sistership, A Division of Full
   Sail Sailing School
Pat Nolan, Owner
PO Box 11156
St. Thomas, USVI 00801
Phone: 809-494-0512

Womanship
Suzanne Pogell, Founder
The Boathouse
410 Severn Avenue
Annapolis, MD 21403
Phone: 800-342-9295
410-267-6661
Fax: 410-263-2036
e-mail: Womanship@aol.com

Women for Sail
Nancy Barnes, President
1035 West Belden/#3
Chicago, IL 60614
Phone: 800-346-6404
773-327-3239
Fax: 773-528-4030

Women's Sailing Adventures
Sherry Jagerson, Owner
39 Woodside Avenue
Westport, CT 06880
Phone: 800-328-8053
203-227-7413

Bibliography

Recommended Reading for Confidence and Preparation

Please note: Some of these books are no longer be in print. Your public library may have them in their collection. Some specialty marine booksellers, such as Armchair Sailor and Columbia Trading, will search for out-of-print titles.

Eastman, Peter, M.D. *Advanced First Aid Afloat.* Centreville, Maryland: Cornell Maritime Press, 1974.

Farrington, Tony. *Rescue in the Pacific.* Camden, Maine: International Marine, 1996.

Gill, Paul G., Jr. *The Onboard Medical Handbook.* Camden, Maine: International Marine, 1997.

Green, Lyndsay. *Babies Aboard.* Camden, Maine: International Marine, 1990.

Hydrographer of the Navy. 3rd ed. *Ocean Passages for the World.* Taunton, England: Hydrographic Department, Ministry of Defence, 1987.

Morgan, Lael. *Woman's Guide to Boating and Cooking.* 2nd ed. New York: Doubleday, 1974.

Neal, John, and Barbara Marrett. *Mahina Tiare*. Friday Harbor, Washington: Pacific International Publishing, 1993.

Norgrove, Ross. *The Cruising Life*. Camden, Maine: International Marine, 1980.

Pardey, Lin. *The Care and Feeding of Sailing Crew*. Middletown, California: Pardey Books, 1995.

Pardey, Lin, and Larry Pardey. *Storm Tactics Handbook*. Middletown, California: Paradise Cay Publications, 1995.

Riley, Dawn, with Cynthia Flanagan. *Taking the Helm*. Boston: Little, Brown and Company, 1995.

Roth, Hal. *After 50,000 Miles*. New York: W.W. Norton, 1977.

Rousmaniere, John. *The Annapolis Book of Seamanship*. New York: Simon and Schuster, 1983.

Rousmaniere, John. "Fastnet, Force 10." New York: W.W. Norton, 1980.

Stevenson, Janet. *Woman Aboard*. Novato, California: Chandler & Sharp, 1981.

US Sailing. *Bareboat Cruising*. Portsmouth, Rhode Island: US Sailing, 1996.

US Sailing. *Basic Cruising*. Portsmouth, Rhode Island: US Sailing, 1995.

US Sailing. *Basic Keelboat*. Portsmouth, Rhode Island: US Sailing, 1995.

Webb, Barbara. *Yachtsman's Eight Language Dictionary*. Dobbs Ferry, NY: Adlard Coles, 1983.

Werner, David. *Where There Is No Doctor*. Rev. ed. Palo Alto, California: The Hesperian Foundation, 1992.

I've included the following two books because they demonstrate two very different cruising relationships. Both couples sailed Cape Horn, a challenging part of the world. But they brought with them very different skills, attitudes, and partnerships. For books about cruising, these titles are just the tip of the iceberg.

Hemingway-Douglass, Réanne. *Cape Horn: One Man's Dream, One Woman's Nightmare*. Bishop, California: Fine Edge Productions, 1994.

Roth, Hal. *Two Against Cape Horn*. New York: W.W. Norton, 1978.

Index

A

adolescents aboard, 79–81
Advanced First Aid Afloat
   (Eastman), 58, 59
air conditioning, 113
amateur radios.
   See ham radios
American Express offices, 91, 93, 94
American Radio Relay League, 95,
   144, 160
Amesbury, Gail, 11, 17, 77, 79, 80–81,
   84, 112, 117, 130
appliances, 154–55
ARRL. *See* American Radio Relay
   League
autopilots, 35–36, 110

B

bad weather, 39–48
basic skills, 21–22, 31, 35, 143–44.
   See also dinghy operation
   learning, 15–21
   practicing, 47–48

bathing, 34, 113, 133–35
Bischoff, Nancy, 30–31, 51, 71, 75,
   79, 80, 81, 88
boats
   appearance of, 54–55
   basics of, 29–30
   gear for, 34–36
   interior layout of, 108–9
   selection of, 28–38
   size of, 30–31
   upkeep of, 38
boat shows, 28, 46
boat units, 108
boredom, 123–32
Bowdish, Gail, 18, 57, 62, 65–66, 67
Brigham Young University high
   school program, 81, 161
British Navy Hydrographic Department
   Ocean Passages for the World, 44
bugs, 156–57
bunks, 32, 112
Burke, Louise, 109, 134, 139

C

Calvert School home-study courses,
76, 161
*Cape Horn: One Man's Dream, One
Woman's Nightmare*
(Hemingway-Douglass), 12
career planning, 98–106
Centers for Disease Control, 61, 161
charterboats, 28
charts, 44–45
children aboard, 70–81
clothes wringer/dough
roller, 113
clothing, 137–38
appropriateness of, 55, 56,
138, 149
Colborn, Barbara, 4–5, 6, 10, 42,
64–65, 92, 119–20, 123, 127,
135, 137, 144
common sense, 55–56
communications, 84, 90–97, 127
electronic, 101
radio, 37, 94–95, 143–44
telephone, 95–96
communication styles, 11–12
courier services, 92–93
cruising services, 160–63

D

Dead Calm (film), 41
dehydration, 47, 66, 75
dental kits, 59–60
destinations, 129–32, 140–46
dinghy operation, 141–42, 150
Dinius, Paula, 4, 12, 43, 44–45, 111,
134, 136–37, 138
drogues, 47–48

E

Eastman, Peter F.
Advanced First Aid Afloat, 58, 59
electrical systems, 110–11, 155
e-mail, 96–97
emergencies
contacts in, 86–87

equipment for, 36–37
medical, 62–63
emergency position-indicating
radiobeacon. *See* EPIRB
employment, 98–106
EPIRB, 36–37, 94

F

family issues, 85–86
Farrington, Tony
Rescue in the Pacific, 41–42
"Fastnet, Force 10" (Rousmaniere),
41–42
FCC. *See* Federal Communications
Commission
fears, 24, 40–43
of bad weather, 39–41
Federal Communications Commission, 94, 95, 144, 160
finances, 91–92
fishing, 78
fitness, 68–69
flare guns, 37
flotilla cruising, 53, 55
foods
for babies, 74–75
for children, 74–75, 77–78
convenience, 152–53
intake of, 46–47
foul-weather gear, 45–46
Francis, Lura, 3–4, 6–7, 12–13, 30,
101, 151–52
freeboard, 36

G

galley, 32–33, 108, 113, 153–57
garbage disposal, 74, 157
grandparenting, 85–86
guilt, 88–89

H

hair care, 135–36
Hampshire, Irene, 30, 53, 76, 77, 80,
81, 104, 112, 158
ham radios, 95, 97, 127, 144

head, 33–34
health concerns, 57–69
  about appearances, 133–39
  adolescent, 80
  child, 73–74
  menopausal, 66–67
  menstrual, 64–65
  pregnancy, 65–66
  premenstrual syndrome,
    64–65
  school-age child, 77
"Health Information for
  International Travel"
  (USGPO), 61
health insurance, 61–62
heating, 113
heaving-to, 47
heeling, 23
Hemingway-Douglass, Réanne,
  82–83, 118
  Cape Horn: One Man's Dream,
  One Woman's Nightmare, 12
home, 107–14
  boat as, 107–9
  leaving, 82–89
  returning, 25, 158–59
homesickness, 84–85

I
iceboxes, 33
immunizations, 61, 73
independence, 141–42
infants aboard, 71–76
information sources, 160–63
  about bad weather, 41–42,
    44–45
Inmarsat-C satellite communication
  system, 97
instructors for sailing, 16–17
International Health Insurance of
  Denmark, 62, 161
International Travelers' Information
  Hotline, 61
inventory reduction, 115–17,
    121–22, 145

J
jealousy, 87
Jewhurst, Nancy, 13, 30, 71, 76, 77,
    78, 79, 111, 112, 128, 132

K
Keelboat Certification Program, 19
KISS principle, 109–10

L
language skills, 55, 56, 58, 141, 142, 149
life jackets, 72–73, 77
lifelines, 72
life rafts, 37
lifestyles, 2–3, 123–32, 158–59
liquor aboard, 54, 56, 129–30, 151
living quarters, 23–24, 31–32
  for school-age children, 78
living standards, 55
logkeeping, 126

M
mail, 90–94
makeup, 136–37
man-overboard procedures, 22–23, 36
marine surveys, 38, 161–62
MARPOL Treaty, 65, 157
Marrett, Barbara, 3, 5, 14–15, 20, 30,
    84–85, 102, 111, 117, 137, 139, 146
MASH. See Medical Advisory
  Systems Hotline
"mayday," 37
McCullough, David
  Path Between the Seas, 145
Medical Advisory Systems Hotline,
    62–63, 161
medical kits, 59–60, 73, 77
medical records, 60–61, 73
medical training, 58–59
mementos, 116, 117, 118, 119–20, 145
menopause, 66–67
menstruation, 64–65
message services, 96
milk, ultra-heat treated, 67, 74–75,
    77, 152

Miller, Patricia, 10–11, 43, 53, 65, 103–4, 112, 117, 129–30, 138, 142–43, 158
modesty, 134
Morgan, Lael, 9, 13, 17, 42, 52, 99, 112
moving aboard, 109–11

N
National Women's Sailing Association
Women's Sailing Resource, 45, 160
Nolan, Pat, 11–12, 16, 18
NWSA. *See* National Women's Sailing Association

O
Ocean Passages for the World (British Navy), 44

P
pace setting, 123–25, 131–32, 146
Pardey, Lin, 2, 4, 10, 19, 20, 27, 30, 40, 41, 52, 53, 54, 58, 67, 99, 111, 120, 121, 138, 144, 158, 159
Path Between the Seas (McCullough), 145
Payson, Nancy, 2, 6, 8, 12, 20, 67, 70–71, 106, 112, 117, 119, 120, 146
personal skills, 144–46
pirates, 51–52
PMS. *See* health concerns, premenstrual syndrome
pocket cruisers, 26
Pogell, Suzanne, 17–18, 20
port life, 128–29
pregnancy, 65–66
preparations
for bad weather, 45–48
for children, 72
destination, 140–46
for leaving home, 82–84, 164–65
medical, 58–63
privacy, 109, 134
for adolescents, 80

Private Patients Plan, 61–62, 161
provisioning, 147–57

R
radio nets, 127, 130
reading, 145–46, 164–65
refrigeration, 33, 78, 155–56
relationships, 9–11, 130–32, 159
controlling, 87–88
Rescue in the Pacific (Farrington), 41–42
Riley, Dawn, 15, 42, 53, 64, 104, 111
Rousmaniere, John
"Fastnet, Force 10," 41–42

S
sabbatical cruising, 102–3
safe deposit boxes, 119
safety
of adolescents, 80
of children, 72–73
of school-age children, 77
Safety-at-Sea Seminars, 162
safety gear selection, 36–37
safety harnesses, 36, 46, 73, 77, 126
sails
reefing, 47
roller-furling, 47
test, 28, 71
schedules, 125–28, 131–32, 146.
See also watch systems
Scherer, Migael, 2–3, 6, 8–9, 10, 52, 102, 113, 117–18, 119, 139
Still Loved by the Sun, 52
schooling
of adolescents, 80–81
home, 76–77
schools, sailing, 17–19, 162
sea anchors, 47–48
sea legs, 63–64
Sea Sense, 18, 162
seasickness, 23, 63–64, 148
Seattle Sailing Foundation, 36
security, personal, 49–56
self-steering systems, 35–36

sex aboard, 138–39
shopping, 55, 149–50
sickness, 57–69. *See also* homesickness
Simon, Michelle, 68
single-sideband radios, 94, 97, 127, 143–44
Sistership, 18, 163
skin care, 67, 136–37. *See also* sun protection
socialization
of children, 75–76
of school-age children, 78–79
SSB radios. *See* single-sideband radios
Still Loved by the Sun (Scherer), 52
storage systems, homebased, 118–21
storms, 24–25
stoves, 33
stowage, 34, 155–57
sunglasses, 74
sun protection, 67–68, 73–74, 136

T
tableware, 155
tests, two-use, 113
toddlers aboard, 71–76
traveling, 146

U
U.S. Coast Guard, 20–21, 62
U.S. Government Printing Office
"Health Information for International Travel," 61, 161

U.S. Power Squadron, 20–21
U.S. State Department, 54
U.S. Sailing Association
Where to Sail, 18–19, 160

V
valuables, 117–18
VHF radios, 94, 127, 143–44

W
Wales, Patience, 4, 11, 19, 20, 27, 30, 40–41, 63, 88, 133–34
watch systems, 24, 47, 125–27
watermakers, 110
water supply, 33, 75, 150
weapons aboard, 53–54, 55
weatherfaxes, 127–28
Werner, David, 58–59
Where There Is No Doctor (Werner), 58–59
Where to Sail (U.S. Sailing Association), 19
winches, 35
wind vanes, 35
Womanship, 17–18, 20, 163
Women for Sail, 18, 163
Women's Sailing Resource (NWSA), 45

Y
yoga, 68